# Braving It

# Braving It

*The gentle art of living boldly*

Diana Davin

Blossie's Books

www.blossiesbooks.com

© 2021 Diana Davin. All rights reserved. No part of this book may be reproduced or transmitted in any form or by any means, electronic or mechanical, including photocopying, recording, or by any information storage and retrieval system, without permission in writing from the publisher.

Published by Blossie's Books
1-201-450-3654
E-mail: info@blossiesbooks.com
www.blossiesbooks.com
ISBN 13: 978-1-891019-51-7

# Also by Diana Davin

*Available in print and ebook format on amazon and barnesandnoble.com*

## Make this book your own
Everyone comes to a book like this at different points. Make this book your own by looking for the ideas that make the most sense for you. Then, go be awesome by using these ideas when, how, and where they fit your unique and beautiful life.

## Disclaimer
Blossie's Books aim to help you open your mind and eyes to an amazing, high potential future and build the life you want. Your results, however, are your responsibility. Blossiesbooks.com does not provide legal, health, or financial advice and does not guarantee the results obtained by readers of its books, blogs, website, or any other materials.

## Privacy
As always, the names I use in my stories have been changed to protect the privacy of my friends and clients.

Welcome to Blossie's Books!

Blossie's Books are for you, beautiful someone, as you wake up to the wildly awesome person you are.

Every Blossie's Book is a quick read of simple ideas for how we can live our lives happy, healthy, sane and more awesome than ever. Read one with your coffee or lunch and start using the ideas right away.

*The Gift of No, Dream Come True, You Know What I ~~Should Have~~ Said?, Simply Irresistible,* and *The Becoming Journal* were just the beginning. Stay tuned, there's so much more to come!

Write to me at diana@blossiesbooks.com. I so want to hear your awesome story!

And thank you, THANK YOU for buying one of Blossie's Books! Wherever you are on your journey to awesome, I'm incredibly happy you're spending some time with me.

Now go be awesome!

# Contents

## Part 1: First things

| | |
|---|---|
| The Story of *Braving It* | 1 |
| Freeing our brave hearts | 31 |

## Part 2: Coming home

| | |
|---|---|
| Relax into honesty | 67 |
| Brave your boundaries | 75 |
| Own your amazing | 89 |
| Find (or create) work you love | 101 |
| Bless this body | 109 |
| Let only love in | 121 |
| Stop explaining! | 135 |
| Shhh...listen! | 145 |
| Face it | 155 |
| Create your joy | 165 |
| | |
| That's all for now! | 177 |

# Part 1: First things

"Yes, here I am returning, the woman who bore herself to the bottom and back.

Who wanted to swim like dolphins, leaping waves and diving.

Who wanted only to belong to herself."

— Sue Monk Kidd
From the Prologue
to her novel,
*The Mermaid Chair*

*BRAVING IT*

# The Story of *Braving It*

> Afoot and light-hearted
> I take to the open road,
> Healthy, free, the world before me,
> The long brown path before me
> leading wherever I choose.
>
> — Walt Whitman
> *Song of the Open Road*

Jo had a mirror. Not in a drawer or off to the side of her desk. But in front of her. Facing her, where she could see it all the time. She happened to be objectively beautiful, and so at first I thought the mirror was just vanity, that she wanted to admire herself all the time.

But as I got to know her, *vain* was probably the last word I'd use to describe Jo. She was smart, humble, and kind, someone who became a good friend. One day, I asked her about the mirror, "Why do you keep a mirror facing you at your desk? It would make me crazy to see myself all day at work!"

"It's there to remind me to be myself in every situation," she said, "to never get caught up in all the bonkers stuff that goes on around here."

Jo wasn't vain. She was just *awesome*.

What made Jo so awesome? Her commitment to being her honest, authentic self in every situation.

A unique, one-of-a-kind *individual*.

## Our unique selves

We spend way too much time second-guessing ourselves, not trusting our intuition, in fact, treating it as suspect because it's not "scientific" or tangible — something that we can weigh or hold in a measuring cup. And we as a society, and even as a world, have been taught to distrust what we can't experience with our five senses, that somehow things that can't be experienced this way aren't real.

But we can blow this apart with some simple facts: love is real, electricity is real, hurt is real — I could keep going, but while none of these things can be measured or seen or smelled, they exist. They are *real*. They don't have a color, a weight, a scent. And still, they are essential to our experience of reality as humans.

Even our very life — the electricity that flows through us while we are alive — heart-pumping-lungs-filling *alive* — is immeasurable. If I weigh 140 pounds and I die, if you weigh me, I will still weigh 140 pounds. My very life, the essence, the electricity that animated me is weightless and formless. It's also *real*. And it, like all the most organic parts of ourselves, isn't something we have to work on. It just is. It's effortless.

It just makes sense then that we need to trust the parts of ourselves that *can't* be measured and know that they are real: our insights, memories, natural talents, hopes, dreams, and our intuition. These are not just fluffy, ethereal, unimportant aspects of ourselves. On the contrary, they are part of what makes us who we are. Taken together, they enable us to be our unique selves.

And, like Jo, we need to trust our uniqueness, live it without apology, and guard it with all our heart.

## Our differences are not an accident!

Since the dawn of time, there's never been anyone with our combination of genetics, brains, fingerprints, experiences, and relationships. We are physically and mentally and emotionally one-of-a-kind (which is both scientifically true and kinda mind-blowing when you sit with it for a while...).

The fact that we are all different just *can't* be an accident! Our differences are the source of our ability to learn from each other, to be stimulated by each other, and through that electricity, to form strong bonds with each other. Our differences are the creative sparks that enable us to learn from each other and to grow (i.e., to change for the better).

Differences of opinion and ways of approaching problems make for stronger, more balanced and fulsome solutions to problems. People with ways of thinking that challenge or complement ours are interesting to us, and in this way, our differences are a magnetic force that draws us toward each other. Differences make us stronger and healthier together.

Our differences also reinforce our individuality and the uniqueness we each bring to the world. They enable us to make one-of-a-kind contributions to our relationships, jobs, communities, even (and maybe especially) when our differences are quirky, eccentric, or idiosyncratic. They enable us to leave positive memories behind in every situation, a fact that no doubt helped write this inscription I saw on a headstone at an old cemetery: "Those never die who leave behind love in the hearts of others."

Given the extraordinary power of our differences, it makes *no sense at all* to spend as much time as we do comparing ourselves to other people: what they have, what they drive, who they're with, their job, education, appearance...*and yet we do!* No one has stood in our shoes, behind our eyeballs and had our one-of-a-kind combination of biology and circumstances, and yet a big part of our life's quest is to shapeshift until we're all the same!

We're constantly looking at everyone else for cues and validation about how to live our lives, what is acceptable, essentially everything that is desirable in a human being. (No judgment here, beautiful someone. I do it too!)

## Isadora

It's always amazing to hear about people who brave their lives naturally, effortlessly. I can't help but wonder what combination of biology and experiences enables them to be so true to themselves, regardless of who they're with or the situation they're in. To have the courage of their own truth, to listen and live by their inner voice, often in spite of some of the loudest and most insistent voices shouting around them — this amazes me.

If you don't know the name Isadora Duncan, it's worth Googling her. Isadora was a choreographer and dancer who performed in the 1920s and 30s. A renegade, she was definitely unconventional, someone we might label rebellious or an instigator. Her interpretive style of dance took on the art of ballet, unmoored it from its restrictive, tightly prescribed movements and combinations and transformed it into a creative art form that told a story full of personal expression. And in this respect, she is often credited with helping to spark the development of modern dance.

Isadora's choreography focused on opening every movement from the heart center. There aren't many, but you can find a few videos of her work being performed. If you watch, right away you'll be able to sense this openhearted way of dancing.

And Isadora lived the same way — heart first. She just put it out there and, as the saying goes, "Damn the torpedoes! Full speed ahead!" Her life was out-of-the-box for the time and included multiple relationships and children with different people. Sadly, she passed away at an early age in a tragic accident, but in the world of dance, her legacy endures.

At a vintage shop a few years ago, I found this Isadora Duncan quote painted on a piece of tile:

*"You were wild once. Don't let them tame you."*

It's hanging in my kitchen where I check in with it literally every day.

Knowing a little about her life now, it's easy to see that this advice from Isadora is completely in character. (And knowing me, it's easy to see why I love her ☺.)

But the quote, especially the last part: "Don't let them tame you"... that just touches a nerve. I don't ever want to sit down, be quiet, and fit in. More than that, I don't want to be told what a happy life looks like when that's so different for each of us. I don't want to be surrounded by people who say things like, "You should be [*fill in the blank*]" or "That's so weird that you don't like..." or "Why don't you just..." or "How could you possibly feel like that?" or "Why would you ever say something like that?" or "You know how crazy that sounds?"

Nor do I want to feel wordless pressure to show up for people or situations that require me to compromise my true self (especially to make it smaller or vanilla so as not to stand out or excel).

I want to *create* a life that makes me and the people I care about happy and healthy. I want to live and work and play joyfully, never performing or being untrue to myself and the people I love. And through that joy, I want to contribute to the world around me, in all creating a life that's as unique as my own fingerprints.

## And yet...*yet*...

For the longest time (like for*ever*), making everyone happy and comfortable has been my life's relentless and unwavering focus. The need to shapeshift in any situation to be sure to put myself last and everyone else first has been a literal fixture in my life, defining the tone and texture of every conversation and relationship I've had for as long as I can remember.

And I do mean *any* situation, and I do mean *everyone* else.

Maybe, beautiful someone, you understand?

A little more (but not too much 😊) detail: in my former life as a communications professional, everything I did was in service of others, to be sure my employer/client was completely satisfied no matter what that took —

If it meant cutting my fees to the bone, *done!*

If it meant taking the blame for a mistake I wasn't responsible for — *you bet!*

If it meant working day and night with no sleep for 72 hours straight to help someone out of a really bad jam they got themselves into — *no problem!*

If it meant being told after working for months on a proposal that the project wasn't going to happen because there was never any budget for it in the first place — *oh, of course I understand!*

If it meant working over vacations, holidays, birthdays, and even in the lounge at my cousin's wedding — *you got it!*

If it meant returning emails from my hospital bed after my C-sections (that's <u>plural</u>) — *sure thing!*

Outside my work life, with friends, in romances, and with extended family especially, everyone else was always right, their needs were more important than mine, boundaries were not a thing, they deserved everything and I deserved nothing in the relationship (except the privilege of being allowed in one). In every conflict, I gave in quickly and often apologized for taking a stand in the first place.

In short, as long as everyone within a ten-mile radius of me was happy, I was good, no matter what that cost me, my family, and the other people I loved.

The idea of speaking up, being honest about my boundaries (or even knowing I could *have* any), having the personal confidence to be honest and real and not feel weird and different (read: wrong and inferior), making my own goals a priority, telling boundary crashers that it's *not* okay — none of this occurred to me for a long, long (long) time. And I'm still not great at any of it — even when someone insults me or cuts me off on the highway or is really rude, my first thought is, "I'm sure I deserved that. Now I just have to figure out what I did to deserve it." (I *swear*.)

All this (this *what*? Lack of confidence? Insecurity? Fear of rejection?), beautiful someone, despite an honors degree from Harvard, years of business experience, marriage, divorce, remarriage, two amazing kids, home ownership, great friends, and hundreds of professional connections. Why haven't I stood my ground? Spoken up? Asked for what I want? Enforced boundaries?

I don't completely know why, though I'm determined to find out, and more important to change for the better (i.e., for the *braver* ☺).

## What I *do* know

I'm learning to do all those things: to speak out, to draw boundaries, to tell the truth, to not care about impressing people, in short, to shield my soul and my heart from the assaults they used to experience every day. I know that "No" can be a complete sentence, that joy is a life strategy, and that it's <u>never</u> too late to begin again.

I've learned strategies for fortifying my insides – the home of my true, unique, one-of-a-kind self. I know in my bones now that I've been entrusted with sharing through my books and my art what I've learned "the hard way," to encourage other people and thus to give them hope and help inspire them. And I know that I am safer now, safe to share all this with you without being afraid of defying a rule or flouting convention or just acting "untamed" to borrow Isadora's imagery.

I really do believe that this is God's great assignment to each of us, beautiful someone. A seed has been planted in each of us that's completely unique for a reason, and that reason certainly isn't to hide its uniqueness. It's to share it, and in doing so, to help other people see things they otherwise wouldn't see, understand things they otherwise wouldn't understand, experience things they otherwise wouldn't experience, be comforted in ways they otherwise wouldn't be comforted.

## Prayers from the dying

At the time the idea for *Braving It* was taking shape in my mind, fueled (as all Blossie's books are in one way or another ☺) by my own heartfelt experiences and those of the people I love, an amazing book crossed my path: *The Top Five Regrets of the Dying*. Written by Bronnie Ware as a series of reflections on her time providing palliative care in people's final days, this amazing book traces the many ways in which Bronnie herself was transformed by the gift of getting to know these people at this time in their lives.

Especially striking is the number-one regret Bronnie heard people share: "I wish I'd had the courage to live a life true to myself, not the life others expected of me." Sitting with that for a moment is nothing less than earth-shattering. Really — to look back and say so late in life, actually at the very end, something this huge about how you spent the gift of your heartbeat was just jaw-dropping to me. That it's possible to feel that after having been given a life to create, that we did the opposite — we didn't create it, but simply *re*-created it based on the experiences of other people, their expectations, their filters, their biases, their goals.

Also interesting is the way in which this is articulated as a matter of *courage* ("I wish I'd had the courage..."). I agree! It *does* take courage to swim against the tide of other people's expectations. In fact, sometimes that may be the most courageous thing we do in our lives. The tide is so strong, there are so many expectations of us, so many opinions of what constitutes a worthwhile life, a successful career, good parenting, plus pressure to have the right kind of car, house, appearance...*this list can go on for 100 pages*!

Sometimes when I look at a person in their 50s or 60s who made a life out of their art, or a Special Education teacher who dedicated their life to taking care of precious special needs children, or an oncology nurse — these kinds of professions fill me with appreciation, respect, and I mean this sincerely: *awe*. Because honestly? I know that choosing these kinds of careers required sacrifice — lots of it. In some cases financial sacrifice, but much more significantly, spiritual sacrifice — like the knowledge that they were creating art that would in all likelihood (at least initially) be harshly criticized and rejected. The need to be able to celebrate the most minute improvements in a special needs student's performance. The peace of keeping a seriously ill person out of pain for just a little while. The stress of dealing with difficult parents and family members who are trying to help but sometimes can't do so effectively. *And still these people stuck to their passions.* They lived according to what gave them a sense of purpose and joy and built a life around it.

They had the courage to brave their lives and their passions and swim upstream against the tides of *same* and *more*. And I isolate those age groups in particular because while the alluring "siren song of more" as author Julia Cameron calls it, was screaming in the background in the 1980s and into the 1990s especially, when these people would have been coming of age, the pressures to "succeed" by making ungodly sums of money however you could, buying a palatial mansion, and driving a luxury car were enormous. The tide pulling them was more like a tsunami.

And so, with humble thanks to Jo, Isadora, and finally Bronnie, I set out to write *Braving It*, a book about finding ways to literally give ourselves permission to *be* ourselves, and then to enjoy our lives from this vantage point — that would be inside out. To savor our uniqueness and enjoy our lives far from the reach of judgment of other people (which is nothing compared to the harsh ways in which we tend to judge ourselves).

Beautiful someone, here's a hug. Now, let's get started!

## The promise of *Braving It*

Imagine the happy/healthy/sane that comes from creating a life true to our unique goals, talents, and passions.

Picture...

Not having to apologize for who we are or what makes us different.

Not having to pretend — anything — so we can fit in or impress someone.

Taking genuine pride in what we're good at and being confident to talk about our talents without worrying that we're making anyone uncomfortable.

Not feeling guilty about what we're *not* good at.

Knowing we're enough as we are.

Being relaxed and comfortable in our bodies, behind our eyes.

Saying *yes* without fear and *no* without guilt.

Being completely in a moment, experience, conversation, new opportunity...unfettered by the stuff we tend to lug around with us (feelings of inadequacy, guilt, unworthiness, thoughts like, "I really should be doing something else," "I wonder if I remembered to sign my tax return," or "OMG, I just remembered the epic fail when I tried this five years ago...").

Not needing the approval of other people.

Believing that we deserve good things to happen sometimes by chance and sometimes because of how hard we work but most important, knowing that there is no cosmic force "out there" that doesn't want us to succeed.

Believing that we deserve to be loved just for who we are not because of anything we did for someone or could potentially do for them.

This is the promise of *Braving It*, beautiful someone. Together, we'll build the strength to tune out the negative voices and genuinely appreciate who we are as unique individuals. We'll build the confidence to be true to the love in our hearts for people we consciously choose to surround ourselves with.

We will learn to love our unique talents and never put these gifts down in any way, especially to make someone else feel comfortable. We'll cultivate the self-love and self-respect that enable us to know our choices are not wrong simply because they may be different from the crowd's or what we see online. We'll discover how to find or create meaningful work we truly love and show up for every day with energy and excitement.

And, so important: we will know that how we look, what brings us joy, what sucks the life out of us, how we want to spend our time... No matter how similar or different they are to everyone else's, these choices are not right or wrong.

They are just one thing: *ours*.

(And in a nod to the miracle of genuine self-respect, when we respect our own choices, we also respect the choices of other people, even when they are the complete opposite of our own. RIP the splintering judgment that pulls us apart from each other.)

## Gabi's story

Once a marketing executive for a financial services company who has since started her own urban landscape design business, Gabi shared this story:

"In the months before I left the world of finance finally and forever, one thing I remember clearly is my daily trip into the office. As an executive, I got to use the indoor parking garage under the building. This was a big perk because everyone else had to park in a giant outdoor lot and walk to the building, sometimes from as far away as a quarter of a mile, even in the snow and rain.

"Still, we all used the same main entrance, and I remember the feeling of walking in the door in my expensive suit and leather bag, feeling isolated and very alone as I headed to my office. I'd look at the people coming to work in comfortable clothes and shoes and smiling. I knew they had jobs that would let them start their day, work through their shift, then go home and spend time with their families. They probably even had time for hobbies and workouts!

"Often they'd be talking to friends and coworkers, holding giant cups of Dunkin' Donuts coffee and just looking comfortable and safe and *happy*. As I thought about what I really wanted in life, these people came to mind as I reflected on the balance in their lives, the delicious coffee, the comfortable shoes and clothes they wore. They just looked so relaxed! And when I compared that to how I felt — tense, scared of stepping out of line with another executive, essentially a complete poser...well, even just remembering makes me feel like crying. I was so miserable."

What began as a seed planted in Gabi's soul those winter mornings as she trekked down the long hallway to her job, took root and began to grow. She became intensely aware of the unhappiness that she felt every day and one day, decided enough was enough.

"It's not that I judge anybody else for what they may choose to do," she said. "Honestly, plenty of my colleagues were happy with what they were doing, the trade-offs that they had made in their work lives for the huge salary, even if that meant less time with their families, an inability to share their honest opinions, and just an overall high-stress environment. To them, it was worth it, and I get that. I just knew for myself that if I kept on the path that I was on, I would pay a very high price – higher than I wanted – just to be able to make more money to buy stuff I probably didn't really want and my kids didn't need anyway."

For Gabi, making a change was not a lightning-bolt revelation. It was gradual and methodical. She traced her feelings as they evolved, then gathered information until one day, a plan took shape and the timing was right. Gabi jumped down every YouTube rabbit hole that could help her start a landscaping business. She even found some local groups meeting at the library to talk about entrepreneurship, what it meant, and the kind of thinking and planning you have to do to start a business (and met some people who actually became future customers!).

As a planner by nature, she came up with a business development strategy, with detail about the kind of projects she really wanted to attract. She took courses on landscape design, then found a niche designing in small spaces for urban property owners.

"As soon as I knew that I was about to begin living a different truth, one much more aligned with my soul, the world began to open up," she said. "The clouds lifted, and I didn't just walk down that hallway anymore. I sprinted down because I knew the time was limited, and I was working actively on a plan to align my life with my heart."

Starting her business wasn't easy. "I had to make some adjustments, honestly — I used to be able to go out and spend on a pair of shoes what I now made in an entire week. But I wouldn't change a thing. I remember going to bed at night with a giant smile on my face thinking, 'I'm broke!' It was the freest I'd felt in a long time. I knew I was following my bliss, I just knew it. For so long I had felt like an imposter in my life. I was working at something that wasn't right for me, like I was pretending to be passionate about the success of a corporation when really, I couldn't have cared less. Again, I'm not saying anything bad about the people who like that work and lifestyle — I'm still in touch with a lot of my marketing friends — but I finally woke up to my true self, and now when I seem excited about a garden design project, I really am!"

## OMG moments

For Gabi change was a slow build into a solid plan, but we've all had moments of pure insight in our lives: you know those times when all of a sudden you just realize something or remember something? And how often does this happen in a moment when we're not even thinking about it? Like walking the dog or taking a shower? And in that moment we feel a charge of energy followed by a lightness, a profound sense of peace, a complete clarity — sometimes with an energetic, "OMG!" or "Oh yeah!" It's like, "That's totally right! I can't believe I didn't think of that before!"

Moments of enlightenment are very important to pay attention to, beautiful someone, whether they're a slow build or a flash of OMG insight. It's in these moments that we open a private door in our souls and take a peek at our true selves, unselfconscious, unguarded, unposed. In these moments, we know that we *know* that we *know* something, and there's no question that it reveals a deep truth with the power to propel our lives forward in remarkable ways.

Listen as real people talk about these moments in their lives:

"For years, like *forever*, I thought I wanted to go into physical therapy, and it took five years to finish my degree. But I was restless all the time. Then, one day I was swimming in this perfectly clear pond, I flipped onto my back and looked at the sky. And I knew — I just knew, that it didn't matter to me what I did, I'd be a barista or scoop ice cream or mow lawns until I figured something out, but I wasn't going to go back to the practice I was working in — I *wasn't*. I gave my notice the next day, and a huge weight lifted off my chest."

"Oh definitely, the day I met my girlfriend. I'd been dating for a long time and had every kind of experience we've all had of knowing, even on a first date, that the person wasn't right for me. But when I met Jana, I knew right away, I mean literally right away, that this was something very different and very great. And I was totally right."

"Well I spent a lot of time sweating the details of whether I could buy a house. I did the math like 200 times, and every time I was just a little bit short, or I would have to give up too much or the house I was looking at just didn't seem like a good investment or it was too far from my parents, my brother, and my work. And then one day I saw my house, and the minute I walked in the door and took one look around, I knew this was *home*. The funny thing is that all of a sudden, all the finances and everything else that I worried about didn't matter anymore. I would just make it work because the house was so right. That was five years ago, I'm still standing, and my brother is still my best friend."

"Yeah, I've got a good one: my 'Everest' was always asking customers to pay me what I was worth. I was just terrified that if I tried to charge them the right amount for my interior design services, they would hire someone else. I ended up being very busy because I had to do a lot of projects just to cover my expenses. My aha! moment came when I was bidding on the design of a brand-new law office. The client, who had been constantly talking about how they had no money for the work, left the room to take a call, and as the door shut behind him a page on the table in front of us flipped open — it was the budget page of one of my competitors' proposals, and it was literally *two times* what I was going to ask for! I looked out the window and I swear everything seemed bright and crystal-clear. 'OMG,' I thought, 'this is the moment.' When the client came back in the room, I gave him an estimate that was actually 10 percent higher than what I had just seen on that paper. And he said yes."

These amazing stories actually bring tears to my eyes. I'm not really sure why I find them so emotional — maybe it's because in my own life I've always hesitated to live courageously, so when I see people who are finally at the point where they can do it, I just want to stand up and scream, "You go, gorgeous!"

And not just them, but everyone around them who until these moments were being cheated out of the real, honest, authentic core of who they really were. The brilliant uniqueness that the world deserves from them. Because beautiful someone, when we keep our honest selves hidden behind layers of performance, people-pleasing, or any other set of self-effacing choices, we're literally cheating the world of our gifts. Also missing: the positive, life-affirming energy of our happiness that I swear, radiates out from us to touch every person and every experience in our lives. It's time we realize all this and begin to change it.

And there's something super-interesting about these moments of enlightenment. There are lots of things we can fake: we can pretend to like a job, a person, a movie, a restaurant. We can even fake a convincing laugh, but OMG moments — they can't be faked. They can't be manufactured. It's like because of the nature of what they truly are, these moments of pure personal honesty can't be phony.

We can trust them.

## The opposite of tough

It's interesting how easy living authentically is, or more to the point, how much *easier* it is than the alternative: struggling to keep our masks on and pretending to be ourselves. It actually takes a lot more energy to pose than it does to be honest and natural. That's why we hear things like, "I felt like a weight lifted off my shoulders," and "I felt like I could finally take a deep breath," and "It was the most freeing decision I've ever made" and "For the first time in months, every muscle in my body relaxed" when someone makes a life-changing choice that (finally) points their life in a new direction uniquely right for them.

Beautiful someone, being brave enough to stop pretending is *literally the opposite of effort.* It's *not* working so hard on our masks but instead relaxing into honesty with a giant exhale. It's putting down the weapons, the bow and arrows and the stones that we throw at other people to judge them when they try to take our masks off.

It's leaving the job we keep because we *so* wanted to love it...but just don't. Ditching the workouts that are not a joy anymore but instead a frantic effort not to exceed a certain number on the scale (beautiful someone, *literally* who cares? Style is an attitude, not a size). Losing the painted-on smile we make ourselves wear when we just don't want to be here, with this person, doing this thing...the smile that's so insincere it actually makes our cheeks twitch.

We stop pretending to believe all the preconceived ideas we formed at the knee of people whose priorities came from a different time, possibly a different set of values, and definitely a different set of circumstances from what we're facing. We turn off the unhelpful voices — and this one's easy, beautiful someone, because this is really within our control — literally just turning them off: unsubscribing and unfollowing the pressure kings and queens who make us feel less than...anything.

And we finally, *finally* relax into ourselves.

## *"A beautiful pie"*

Take a look in your private inner mirror. What do we see? For myself, I'd like to say I see a becoming person, involved in life and loving people, a patch of gray hair that showed up during a divorce that's getting harder to hide. A good mom and friend who's also a fitness junkie, someone who loves gardening and tapestry weaving. A person whose balance of solitude and socializing leans more toward solitude, but who would be lost without her friends and her family. A woman who practices gratitude and humility, who gives and accepts kindness and radiates calm confidence. And maybe most of all, a human being absolutely addicted to hope who happily owns all of the above.

I'd *like* to say all this, but what I just described is myself on a really good day. A day when the sun is shining, everyone is being kind, my house is organized, I've written a chapter that I feel great about, I've gone for a long run in the woods, and I haven't eaten an entire bag of cheese doodles. It would also be on a day when I feel confident about Blossie's Books and everything I hope to achieve with them, that I'm helping the people (including you, beautiful someone).

Truth: a lot of times I jump on circumstances, run on feelings, speak without thinking, vent with too much abandon and then feel massive regret the next time I look at the person I treated like my verbal punching bag. I make mistakes. Say yes when I shouldn't. Say nothing when I should speak up. Waste time online. Buy too much yarn and paint and expensive drawing paper.

And I know I need to own all this too, the grief along with the joy, but maybe in a more positive way. I need to hug it all in, know that it's all part of me, and that's it's okay. That my "golden days" are mixed in with my "brass days," that my life is full and empty, great and tough, clean and messy, busy and lonely, confident and awkward, and yes, that's exactly the way it's meant to be.

Loving ourselves is loving *all* of ourselves because unless we do, we don't. And personal courage can feel very out of reach. Grammy-winning artist Sara Bareilles wrote these lines for her song, *She Used To Be Mine*:

> *She's imperfect but she tries*
> *She is good but she lies*
> *She is hard on herself*
> *She is broken and won't ask for help*
> *She is messy but she's kind*
> *She is lonely most of the time*
> *She is all of this mixed up*
> *And baked in a beautiful pie*

Beautiful someone, we are *whole* human beings, and that means we are good and not always good, smart and loopy, kind and indifferent, thoughtful and selfish — we are all of these things, so we need to embrace them all. We can't live honestly and authentically if we don't. As Sara Bareilles also said: "I think there's so much honor and integrity and beauty in being able to be who you are."

This way, we learn from our brass days and move the needle toward more golden days. The right attitude is, "So that happened. I didn't like seeing myself react that way. Gonna work on that."

And we move on. We don't live in regret. We don't beat ourselves up. We don't define ourselves as less than smart or cruel or selfish. We just realize that all of that is the full package of who we are, and there is room for us to learn and grow and get better.

So, unlike in the past, I notice my golden days. I know I'm capable of them. And now I'm uncomfortable when I see myself getting brassy, operating in ways I want to move beyond. And I know that discomfort is progress, even if that's clear only to me.

Paint a portrait of yourself on a golden day for you. Then keep this image, this beautiful becoming person, in mind as a reminder of what you're capable of.

## Nothing to prove; nothing to fake

*When we stop living for other people's opinions, we start living the life <u>we're</u> made for.*

I wrote this sentence 10 minutes ago, and I've been staring at it ever since. In my heart I know it's true, I just don't know what it means exactly.

What *is* the life that each of us is made for? We are all different — our one-of-a-kind combination of parents, grandparents, great-grandparents, great-great-... (etc.), our life experiences, even our fingerprints have never existed before. And so each of our lives will be just as unique. We've each been given an original set of circumstances, relationships, and talents that, taken together, form our identity and gifts which in turn have a unique influence on other people and enable us to leave a legacy behind.

And before you start thinking, "Who me?"— i.e., that there's nothing really special about you, that you're not going to leave any kind of legacy, that your life is just so ordinary that having an impact isn't something you're uniquely destined for, I'm going to challenge you: literally *every* interaction you have with other people has an impact. You are influential whether it's obvious and tangible (projects at work, raising your kids, creating your art, being involved in your community) or not-so-obvious (the kindness you showed to someone who really needed it, the person you let in on the highway, the smile you gave or returned, the time you let someone else's mistake go and didn't make a giant deal out of it, the compassion and good manners you teach your children).

Big and small, obvious and subtle, tangible and intangible, everything we do has both an impact and a longer-term ripple effect, whether we're conscious of it or not.

Beautiful someone, I've written lots of books, tons of blogs, built a YouTube channel, and more. As of this writing I haven't gotten a lot of feedback or sales or subscribers. But still I know that my words, written as they are in love and complete sincerity, are reaching people. Sometimes just my family, sometimes people in my community, sometimes when I just talk about my ideas with the person next to me in yoga class — but I know, I *know* in my bones, that I have helped.

And you too. Your smile, your wave of the hand that says, "No worries — it was no big deal! Please don't apologize!" made a difference to someone. Your work, your children, your example, your healthy choices made visible to other people have encouraged and inspired them in some way. We are all influential, whether we're conscious of it or not. We all have an impact that reaches beyond our private lives and lasts long after we've left the room.

## What is the life we're made for?

Back to the original question: *What is the life we're made for?* We're here with lots of other people, so simple logic dictates that we're not just here for ourselves. What brings us a quality of joy and fulfillment personally that lets us create the life, make the impact, and leave the legacy we're made for?

Courage.

Specifically, the courage to understand and then live in alignment with our passions. To literally brave ourselves by *being* ourselves completely. Especially, as Lao-Tzu wrote in the *Tao Te Ching*, in a world filled with "sharp edges" and "twisted knots."

Beautiful someone, we need the courage to understand our passions, respect them as unique, and live them.

"I've always done that," a woman at the gym told me one day. "I always spoke up for myself and never took crap from anyone." And she looked it: beautiful and confident, and you know what else? Really likeable. You didn't like her less because she was confident and self-assured. You liked her more for it.

But honestly, I think she's the exception.

Most of us *don't* speak up. We judge our passions as different and somehow wrong. We struggle to fit in. To be "normal." It would be great to say this is changing, and maybe it is slowly, but we live in a world where different has too often equaled wrong. Weird. Scary. Something that needs to stay hidden and be repressed.

Take it from someone who has a very small circle of very close friends, who loves to be alone, drinks maybe once a year, is too easily hurt, can study a single flower petal for an hour, is intensely private, would rather read anything on paper instead of on a screen, talks too often like a professor, and okay (really) doesn't like Christmas (I *know*). Oh boy, I am *weird*.

Why *don't* we speak up? Maybe more positively, what combination of circumstances, experiences, and genes enables someone to be comfortable on the edges or even completely outside what's considered normal? And maybe that's not even the point. Maybe we just need to brave our lives for what they are and who we are. No matter where we came from, what we've been through, what we're going through.

And beautiful someone, lest we fret that we just are not brave, please remember this passage from *Yes Changes Everything*:

> You know what, though? We think of courage as something we have or don't have. "I just don't have the courage" or "I'm just not brave" or "[He/she/they] are just braver than I am." But I don't think courage is something we necessarily *have*. Most times, courage doesn't just bubble up from a well somewhere inside us and move our feet forward or vibrate our vocal cords or poke us in the ribs so we magically raise our hand.
>
> After a courageous choice, we don't look back and say, "I decided I was going to tap into my courage reserves. My

tank was 80 percent full, so I had enough to get me through this decision."

## On purpose

Courage is much more deliberate and on-purpose, much less spontaneous and natural. (And if it isn't deliberate and on purpose, sometimes even gritty, I think, it's not actually courage!)

So courage isn't something we *have* — it's something we *show* by being willing to take a chance. Sometimes even with our eyes closed. We just, just, just let our feet leave the ledge and trust that our cape will pop open and let us fly.

Courage is *conscious*, a deliberate choice.

> It's saying yes to the job we don't feel 100 percent ready for because we know no matter how afraid we feel, it's the right decision.

> It's the decision to speak up about injustice when staying quiet feels safer and definitely less complicated.

> It's the choice to raise our shaking hand to volunteer for a tough project when we'd be much more comfortable grabbing a glass of wine with friends.

> It's signing the mortgage we know is going to put a crimp in our mad money for a while but is, in every other way, the right long-term investment.

It's walking up to introduce ourselves to someone we want to meet even though we're facing a better than 50/50 chance of rejection.

It's writing books with no guarantee that anyone will want to read them ☺.

When we operate with this quality of courage — the kind we don't wait to feel — we're acknowledging that yes is a chance: things may go well, they may not, or maybe a little bit of both:

> Yes to a marriage: a lasting commitment to one person — from blue skies to tornadoes and back again (and again).

> Yes to a child: a lifetime and beyond of being completely devoted to another human being down to our bone marrow through every age and stage.

> Yes to a mortgage: 15 or 30 years out into the future, when the money flows — and when it doesn't.

> Yes to a career choice, especially one that involves a certification or degree: years of money and effort.

> Yes to a kitty or puppy: 12+ years and who knows how many chewed chair legs and torn up sweaters and rugs.

> Yes to a job change: leaving what's known, whether we love it or not.

Courage is our feet moving forward, our hand dialing the phone, our fingers typing the email, our mouths curving into a shaky smile, our booties firmly planted in a chair outside someone's office when they've ignored every one of our emails and calls ...when we don't feel like doing any of those things, and especially when they scare the bleep out of us!

This means that the yes that changes everything *does* take courage, but we can't wait around to feel it.

Courage doesn't mean we *feel* brave. It means we *act* brave. We do it without waiting for our feelings to catch up and trust that the feelings will follow.

## And so finally, *inner peace*

*I'm slowly learning that even if I react, it won't change anything, it won't make people suddenly love and respect me, it won't magically change their minds. Sometimes it's better to just let things be, let people go, don't fight for closure, don't ask for explanations, don't chase answers and don't expect people to understand where you're coming from. I'm slowly learning that life is better lived when you don't center it on what's happening around you and center it on what's happening inside you instead. Work on yourself and your inner peace and you'll come to realize that not reacting to every little thing that bothers you is the first ingredient to living a happy and healthy life.*

*— Rania Naim*

There's so much we don't know. Personally, I don't know the science behind the color of the sky or how electricity works or why water expands when it freezes. But I do know that life is better lived when it's not focused on the maelstrom happening around us but instead on a quiet inner peace inside us. It's just logic. Focusing on the maelstrom and trying to shapeshift to accommodate it just makes us well, maelstrommy, which has got to be another word for *crazy*.

Plus, we can only really work on ourselves and our inner peace — these are the only things we can truly control anyway.

So that sounds good, plausible even. But we still need strategies. In *Braving It*, let's walk together on a path to living bravely, authentically, and for real.

Wishing you only good things,

— Diana

## Freeing our brave hearts

> It's time to start something new and trust the magic of beginnings.
>
> — Meister Eckhart

This is one of my favorite quotes from theologian Meister Eckhart. An entire chapter of *The Becoming Journal* is built around it. The best part is *trusting the magic* because there is real magic in trust, especially in trusting our true selves — our honest thoughts and dreams, unrefracted through prisms that belong to other people, online pressures, the past...in general, ideas and values that don't belong to us. Every time we trust ourselves, we have proven to the world, but much more important to ourselves, that we are brave.

Beautiful someone, I have yet to see *trusting the magic* lead to anything but good outcomes in someone's life, sometimes even amazing breakthroughs.

Still, we need a starting point.

So let's go way back. As children, we're nothing but brave. We speak our minds, ask for (*demand* ☺) what we want, cry out loud, jump in puddles, squish scrambled eggs in our tiny fists (because how else can we throw them at the ceiling fan?), fingerpaint with mud, spaghetti sauce, chocolate pudding, and occasionally, actual paint. Our brave hearts are free, unafraid, and wildly expressive.

But then, something happens. We're told to "grow up," stop making a mess, use our inside voice. Nothing wrong with all this...at some point, we need to start acting with concern for the people around us who for some strange reason, may not want scrambled eggs in their ceiling fans or appreciate our ear-piercing screams of frustration over a broken toy. We learn respect and become well-socialized humans.

Somehow though, socialization inevitably goes too far, and instead of just making us aware of other people's feelings and how our actions affect them, every energetic, creative, honest impulse we have gets shut down...

"Shhhh! You are so loud."

"No one cares, Claire! Just keep your opinions to yourself, okay?"

"Art? So *that's* what you call it."

"What's wrong with leaving it the way it is? OMG, you are *so* high maintenance!"

One by one, comments like these pile up into a brick wall we get stuck behind. In the beginning, our authentic selves jump and yell and wave our arms behind the rising wall ("Hey, you know what I think?" "Guys wait, I have a better idea!" "Um, anybody else think that's just dead wrong?" "Look, I created this!" "Hello? Anybody?"), but eventually, all this stops.

The wall's gotten too high. We are now not just self-aware; we are painfully self-conscious. We quiet down and "fit in."

## We, the bulldozer

Beautiful someone, that brick wall holding us back from living honestly and bravely isn't tangible, but it is real. Really real. And in some ways, even more formidable than actual physical bricks.

> It's portable, so it comes with us into every situation we face.

> It's personal, custom-designed to shut us down in ways only we understand.

> It has reinforcements in the form of social pressures and people who have a stake in keeping us small, scared, and tucked away.

> It becomes so much a part of us that we don't even know it's there, preventing some of the best people and opportunities from ever reaching us.

> After being stuck behind it for a while, we don't even know what an honest reaction from ourselves feels like. We believe that the small, scared, and tired person trapped behind the wall is actually us. (It. Is. Not.)

In every conceivable way, this wall is a monster obstacle to a happy, healthy, sane life. It gets in the way of everything, especially the head space and clear light we need to move forward, bravely inviting anything fresh and new and unexplored into our lives.

Physical obstacles that block our way forward are obvious: we look around and see tons of stuff, things we thought were a good idea once but either never worked or no longer work, extra of everything or anything. My friend Angelique buys jar after jar of mustard, her fridge and cabinets are full of them (she thinks ☺), because she so unorganized and cluttered that she's always afraid she's going to run out.

Physical clutter is just too much of anything, like leggings, different kinds of coffee, hand cream, candles (guilty on all fronts!), plus anything we keep long after it's too small or too big or too torn or too out-of-date or broken beyond repair. All this stuff saps our energy because it has to be moved, dusted, insured, repaired, and *blah blah blah*...just clutter!

The good news about physical clutter is that we can snap open a contractor bag and drop it in with a gleeful *buh-bye!*

On the other hand, spiritual obstacles like our brick wall of hyper-socialization are harder to deal with. But deal with them we must! We've got to run a bulldozer through the unique types of obstacles that keep us from taking courageous action and braving our lives.

The sooner we knock those brave-blocking bricks out of the way, the sooner we start our journey to live-out-loud courage.

## Brave-blocking obstacles

We've made ditch lists before, beautiful someone, you and I. We did it in *Yes Changes Everything*, covering everything from old sandals to opinions in need of a *huh?*

There are a lot of candidates for brave-blocking clutter, but let's zero-in on two of the biggest:

1. *Unhealthy relationships.* When we're in relationships that are not edifying and uplifting but instead just the opposite (they pull us down, make us feel hopeless, anxious, scared, and/or sad), we can easily start to question ourselves (our goals, our hearts, our true motives, and our best intentions). Unhealthy relationships spark bad feelings and pull us into circumstances that don't reflect who we are and what we're capable of. They keep us stuck and even afraid of change, definitely not healthy for our brave.

2. *Bad memories.* Good memories are stabilizing and enriching forces in our lives. Bad memories, on the other hand, are emotional bricks that do nothing but weigh us down with past failures and embarrassments. They make us question our abilities or remember times in our lives when we were not at our best. They make us afraid to try new things. And they definitely cause us to distrust the goodness and power of our true selves.

## To start with unhealthy relationships

Full disclosure: this section started as a bunch of lists about how to spot the unhealthy relationships in our lives (from narcissists to naysayers) that block our brave. But literally every time I got up before dawn to write this material, I felt...I think the technical term is *icky*, like I didn't want us jumping into a deep exploration of anger and negativity. It bugged me to think that one of our books, beautiful someone, the ones we share to make life more positive and healthy, would be weighed down with that much sad energy.

So I deleted it all and started fresh. Which ended up being easy because I realized it was possible to talk about these relationships much more economically. There was no need to detail each one on its own. (Un?)fortunately ☺, they have a lot in common.

The relationships I'm talking about — the kind that we need to separate ourselves from or (even better) not get involved with in the first place — have many similarities. And those very similarities are what enable us to recognize them as our intuitive superpowers tell us something isn't right. That intuition talks to us in feelings and nudges that we *absolutely* need to pay attention to. In fact, not just pay attention but *trust* and *honor* as some of the most reliable relationship guidance we receive in our lives.

The people we choose to be in relationships with, more to the point, the people we spend our time with, share our hearts and our thoughts and ideas with, open up to about our hopes and fears...we are incredibly vulnerable to these people and so we need to choose them with great care.

And when they reveal themselves to be damaging to our happy/healthy/sane (and as a result, to our ability to live bravely as our true selves), we need to move away from them. Whether we remove ourselves physically or psychically or both, these relationships *have no place* in our authentic lives. In the words of Prince Harry as he described the choice to distance himself and his family from the unrelenting pressures of royal life, "The relationship now is...space."

We need to walk away from relationships that on balance and over time don't add positive energy to our lives, the ones that don't make us feel loved and accepted. The ones that take our energy not just for a period of time when someone may need us, but *all the time*. The relationships that just draw our life force away from what we want to be doing and should be doing with our one precious life. We need to realize that there are some people who will be in relationships for what they can *get*, without concern for what they *give* or how they make other people feel.

## As a broad brush...

Relationships to avoid or move away from are the ones that block our brave by making us feel bad about ourselves, our ideas, goals, or potential. With the possible exception of our children or life partner, to whom we have deep, abiding responsibilities, it is unwise to engage or stay in relationships that make us feel any combination of: uncomfortable, anxious, guilty, scared, frustrated, angry, insecure, or inadequate...

> People who make us feel like emotional detectives ("I wonder what he/she is feeling today? Why would they act like that? What could I have said that would make them so upset? Or maybe they're not upset, just anxious? Or it could be stress...")

> People we can't be honest around, for whom we must make ourselves smaller or less capable in order to make them comfortable (read: *nonthreatened*).

> People who just exhaust us, emotionally and/or physically.

People who constantly leave us feeling uneasy, as if we're sure we've done something wrong but have no idea what it could be.

People who have a Library of Congress-worthy catalog of all of our weaknesses and mistakes that they look up and trot out every time we are going to eclipse them in some way or make some positive progress in our lives that may move us away from them.

People who are expert at disarming us when we're justifiably angry at them, often by making fun of our strengths ("Oh, here comes the college vocabulary…" "Look at you, staying so calm all the time." "Why do you have to be so positive? It's so phony!")

For sure, relationships go through choppy times, and any relationship can be frustrating at times. There's no need to give up on someone just because the relationship hits a rough spot or a painful growth spurt (e.g., a romantic relationship where you're getting to know each other or a friendship that changes when someone moves away and we have to learn to be close to them at a distance). The problem is when some or all of these feelings predominate the time we spend with someone or constantly preoccupy our thoughts about them, even when we're not together. This is when we may need to take a closer look and maybe a step (or 10 steps) away.

And as a quick side note: we've got to be especially careful about the impulse to actually help people who treat us like this. We are kind, supportive people by nature and so, often we want to help, believe we can make things better, and have endless faith in people, no matter what they do. But especially if the goal is to help them see the light or correct their misperceptions, we can't make people change. We can refuse to accept their behavior and reject their treatment of us, but only they can change themselves, and only if they want to.

No matter how hard we try, *our efforts to change other people will not work.*

## Intuition is genius

In *Yes Changes Everything*, I wrote that,

> Our intuition is a form of genius...I've seriously got to put turning off my brain and trusting my gut high on the list of lessons I wish I'd gotten much earlier in my life. Specifically, to trust that when my stomach is twisting or just giving me that feeling of *yech*, it's talking to me, and this purity of communication, its simplicity, its wordlessness, its inability to make excuses, is often so much smarter than I am in my head. We have both head and heart (intellect and intuition) because we're supposed to use both in our decision making.

To tap into this genius, let's start paying close attention to how the people in our lives act at key moments. Like when we:

- Set a boundary for the first time with them
- Enforce an existing boundary
- Are excited about something
- Accomplish something
- Fail at something
- Bring up something we're passionate about
- Disagree with them
- Agree with them

- Share a new idea with them
- Make a positive suggestion about something they're working on
- Are not available for them
- Say no to them

At these times, are they respectful, supportive, open-minded...or maybe none of these?

Let's also notice...

- How much complaining they do...about their aches and pains and taxes and real estate prices and interest rates, and the general "unfairness" with which they think they're treated
- How they react when they don't get their way
- If we feel defensive as if we're always doing something completely wrong or just not quite right
- If they consistently shirk responsibility, as in: nothing bad is ever their fault
- If they refuse to acknowledge that we've changed and grown, instead treating us like some outdated version they're holding on to
- Whether they keep a long (long) list of the things other people *haven't* done for them
- If they're there for others or just totally absorbed in their own lives
- How they respond to positive ideas for healthy change

Another telling feeling to absolutely trust: how do we feel *after* being with them, are we energized, relaxed, guilt-free, safe, confident, inspired, and just in general, filled with positive feelings and memories of the time together...or maybe not?

Do they approach differences they see in other people (opposing ideas, worldviews, jobs, lifestyles, diets...) with respect and genuine interest or skepticism and annoyance at having their own opinions challenged?

## And one more

How do we feel after we *haven't* been with them for a while: eager to see them soon, or relieved that we haven't had to deal with them, maybe even healthier spiritually and even physically in their absence?

This is an important question, beautiful someone, and a time when we truly need to trust our intuitive genius, because when we're with someone, we don't always think clearly. They may be on their best behavior on a given day or when we're in a group with other people. And everyone has good qualities as well as not-so-good ones. Together with someone, we may (because we are incurable optimists ☺) only see the good.

With the benefit of distance, we gain perspective. This is the chance to really and truly listen to our intuition because if after being with someone we consistently feel drained or guilty (especially if it's unclear what we are feeling guilty *about*), unsure what they really want from us, incapable of keeping up with them or keeping them happy, inadequate, angry...and this is a pattern (like most of the time thinking about them brings up these kinds of feelings), that's a relationship we need to take a hard look at.

## Brave-blocking

The costs of being in low-quality relationships are truly enormous and stand solidly in the way of our ability to live boldly, true to our authentic selves.

To start with the physical cost: the strain of being in a relationship with someone who drains our energy and causes us to question ourselves has real-body consequences: stomachaches, headaches, neck and shoulder pain, poor eating, lack of motivation to exercise...all these and more are symptoms of the stress caused by painful and difficult relationships. Sometimes, our bodies cry the tears that our eyes do not.

There are also spiritual costs. Poor quality relationships, especially if they are influential to us, can cause us to look through a lens that distorts our beautiful lives, leaving us to question our worthiness, dreams, ideas, self-confidence, and even our value as a human being.

*Yes Changes Everything* went into detail about how space in our lives is *privilege*, something we give to people we can trust or more to the point, people who consistently show themselves to be trust*worthy*. The door to our brave hearts can't be wide open to anyone who wants to enter, especially when their intentions are not loving or positive.

So for example, we need to guard our precious ideas and enthusiasm from naysayers because sometimes in order to live bravely, we have to close our eyes, jump, and trust that the net will appear. But if naysayers have convinced us of all the things that could go wrong, our feet will never leave the ground.

Naysayers know how to absorb all the optimism around them and make us feel hopeless. No matter what the idea is, they can find 100 reasons why it's not possible, it's not a good idea, and somehow wanting it is a waste of time because it's beyond our abilities to achieve. These are pessimists of the highest order with a serious stake in maintaining the status quo. They don't like new things so they're not going to like our out-of-the-box idea or unique approach or stretch goal. On the contrary, they will see all of these as threats that need to be taken down as quickly as possible. No matter how strong or immune to naysayers we think we are, their energy affects us — it just does.

Guilt-trippers are another example. If we spend time with people who are happy to offload accountability for their own mistakes and problems onto us, we risk being blamed for everything that's happening to them. Eventually, we may buy-in to the idea that we alone are responsible for their unhappiness, even when we have nothing at all to do with what's happened to them. Result: we're overwhelmed with guilt and then frozen and fearful in our own lives, unable to brave a hopeful and positive future.

## My heart to yours…

Relationships take a lot of energy, which is fine and even good, *as long as* that energy is being invested in relationships that *add to our lives* and *enable us to add to other people's lives* — relationships that on balance and over time give as much as they take. This is the essence of healthy relationships, as opposed to relationships that are just a slow drain on our life spirit, the ones that aren't edifying to us, but instead just depleting.

When we think about the people in our lives, especially those allowed access to our hearts and souls, it's imperative that these relationships are characterized by open-mindedness and respect. Beautiful someone, these are not extras or nice-to-haves. They are *musts*.

My heart to yours: stay away — far away — from people who exhibit these behaviors. They are not being honest or real. We are not a friend, lover, employee, or family member to them. We are an asset, a prop, a project, and sometimes, a necessary evil. Poor-quality relationships can only change us, and by that I mean, at the extreme, destroy us, and definitely our ability, or even desire, to brave our beautiful lives as our true selves. We won't even know who we are anymore, much less have the energy and courage to live authentically. We will leave these relationships feeling scared, incredibly guilty, lost, disconnected, and undeserving of good or positive things.

If you recognize these behaviors in a relationship, end it. Because one of the most important things to realize about low-quality relationships is that they won't change. Certainly, *we* will never change them. And trying to, especially when it takes the form of "helping them be better," is part of a cycle of energy- and spirit-killing codependence.

Though it's incredibly hard to admit this (hope addict that I am), in these relationships, hope can actually be toxic. As we go back into these low-quality relationships hoping they will change, again and again, we lose time, energy, and spirit.

This is a true guard your heart moment. We need to confidently and decisively move away from relationships that pull us down or make us feel fearful, guilty, or stuck in place. There is no other way. We need to recognize what we're dealing with, move physically away if we can, unfollow, block, even change our phone if we have to.

And if we can't, because they're either work relationships that can't be changed right away or family relationships you just can't avoid, have the most superficial of relationships with them. Psychically (i.e., mentally and emotionally) disengage with these people. Do your utmost to limit contact and do not get involved in conversations, projects, get-togethers, or any other interactions. If possible, eliminate alone time with them and no matter what, never sit down for a heart-to-heart.

## Grey rock

Focus in on a key word here: *disengage.*

Disengaging is staying emotionally distant and shutting down our vulnerability to someone. For people recovering from narcissistic abuse, this is sometimes called the "grey rock" technique. It means being about as interested and involved as grey rock would be, i.e., just *blah*. So we don't answer baiting or deliberately confrontational questions. We don't make suggestions or share ideas with them. And we absolutely, definitely, without question, *don't* share personal information of any kind.

We minimize conversation, just nodding with apparent understanding and saying noncommittal, non-engaging things like:

- "Oh gee."
- "Really?"
- "I see what you're saying."
- "Wow."
- "Umm hmmm…"
- "Could be…"
- "That's a possibility."

We answer confrontational questions or statements like, "I thought I told you to…" or "Didn't you once say…" or "I thought we agreed…" or "Isn't it true that…" or "Remember that time you made a fool of yourself when…" with vague indirection:

- "You bet!"
- "Oh, that's yesterday's story. Today's different."
- "It's a new day!"
- "No, not at all."
- "...." (**i.e., silence*)

## Bad memories

*Finish every day and be done with it.*
*You have done what you could;*
*some blunders and absurdities crept in;*
*forget them as soon as you can.*
*Tomorrow is a new day.*
*You shall begin it serenely and with*
*too high a spirit to be encumbered*
*with your old nonsense.*

— Ralph Waldo Emerson

Our memories are precious. For sure, they are part of what makes each of us unique. No one has ever experienced life at the time and place with the family and talents and experiences and friends and fingerprints that we have.

Memories that are positive and supportive are very grounding. They give us a great sense of stability. In them, we find the lessons that help us reach higher as we grow stronger. In fact, memories are some of our greatest teachers as we learn what works and what doesn't.

In hindsight, we can see clearly what moved us forward toward our unique purpose...and what didn't. Memory is critical for protecting ourselves as we discover what's safe and what isn't, who is nurturing to be around and who isn't. In this way, memory is literally a life-saving adaptation (so we as a species know not to eat the red berries on a holly tree that even the birds won't touch...know what I mean?).

Good memories give us a sense of place and belonging. Stories passed from generation to generation help children know they have a history. They're not alone, and they didn't just drop here out of nowhere. Our children love to remember their past. "Mama, tell me about the time I saved the baby bee," "Mama, what was it like when you were a kid? Am I like you were?" The success of services like *23andme* and *ancestry.com* are evidence of our longing to know our own history — the true stories of our past that have helped make us who we are now.

Our own memories connect us to our family and friends. How often are we sitting at holidays watching videos of ourselves as kids, cracking up? A memory breaks free from the back of my mind — something I haven't thought about in years — and I turn to my sisters and say, "Remember the time we spread a blanket out on floor in the den and ate a whole box of confectioner's sugar with spoons?" The memories we share with friends are the ties that bind us together forever. (Who stayed up all night with us cramming for an exam? Who listened to the story of the world's worst breakup? Who had a baby at the same time and compared notes with us about everything from morning sickness to cravings to labor?)

We can debate whether our ability to remember, savor the past and learn from it, to use it to grow in understanding, awareness, empathy, and confidence, are uniquely human. (I for one believe the beautiful animals in my life possess some of these abilities. Yes, including my cat Blossie in Blossie's Books

☺!) Regardless, they do make us uniquely *us*. One-of-a-kind individuals.

Good memories build us up, remind us of our strengths and who we are as human beings. They show us who and what we can count on. They ground us in our heritage and our families.

This very power is precisely what puts a certain quality of memory on our list of bricks that block our brave. Specifically, *bad* memories...

...the ones that don't teach helpful lessons, but instead make us cringe, feel unworthy or inadequate.

...the ones that splinter our relationships with people we care about.

...the ones that make us feel *guilty* — not the "good" kind of guilt that's our conscience telling us we're accountable and can learn something from a situation that we can constructively apply in the future, but instead the kind of guilt that only makes us feel bad and incapacitated to make positive change. This is the kind that just sticks around, without ever turning into constructive action.

Unworthy, guilty, bad...you get the drift. These feelings serve no positive purpose. All they do is make us feel hopeless about the future.

Memories that are purely self-destructive easily find their way onto the pile of bricks we need to get rid of in order to live boldly and honestly. These icky memories are a weight that keeps us stuck in the most negative and unsupportive elements of the past. They're not grounding. They're not instructive. They never morph into constructive action.

Bad memories also cause us to slap unhealthy labels on ourselves:

- "I'm not great with words."
- "I'm the most unorganized person."
- "I'm pretty lazy."
- "I can't make conversation."
- "I'm always late."
- "I'm a bad cook."

None of these is a permanent condition. *Not one.* We can work on any or all of them if we want to. We can organize our lives. Get up early or stay up late to get more done. Study ways to talk to anyone at any time about anything. Choose to be early for appointments. Look up a few simple recipes and learn to cook.

## Let's fix this

Bad memories block our brave by making it seem scary to live boldly because we remember a time when we did just that or tried something simply because we wanted to or we thought it would be good for us, and things did not go well. Rather than seeing these as truly valuable one-of-a-kind learning opportunities, we see them as signs from the universe that this is what will always happen when we try something new.

A big problem with bad memories is that they can become part of us on a cellular level. They can make us think they represent who we truly *are*, when in reality, they're just recollections (sometimes vague, sketchy ones) of something that happened once.

They are **not**, beautiful someone (and let's get this truth down into our beautiful bones), who we *are*.

We are so much more powerful and smarter than our bad memories make us out to be. We are bigger than our mistakes, missteps, fibs, regrets, unfortunate choices (or as a shorthand, the *past*) — and when we allow our past to limit our future, well the bad news is it blocks our ability to brave our lives.

If we say them often enough, and we allow other people to say them about us (and even, *gasp* if we agree with them when they do), unhealthy labels sure sound permanent. They keep us stuck and make us hesitant to venture into new territory.

And they make us afraid.

Afraid to try something new because well, remember that time we tried something like this, and it was an epic fail?

Doubtful about whether we could ever raise a hand for a new project or post for an open role at work because the last time the assignment/position felt like such a stretch that we choked in the interview.

Hesitant to start any new endeavor because well, we've convinced ourselves that we're unorganized, unmotivated, lazy, and chronically late.

Dreading the day when we might want to reach out to a new person because, well, remember all those awkward moments when we did that, and we ended up wanting to run and hide forever?

Afraid, doubtful, hesitant, dreading...these are not the thoughts underpinning the brave and bold lives we want to live!

So let's take a metaphorical sledgehammer to the brave-blocking bricks called bad memories:

- The long-over dead-end relationship and all of its associations and experiences
- The job that was just a mistake from the jump
- The holiday with extended family that turned into an embarrassing heated debate about politics
- Any cringe-inducing ways we used to talk, think, spend our time, look for relationships...
- The times we didn't show up for something when we should have because we just didn't realize how important it was until later
- Our first efforts at *anything* – long before we were good at it and ready for primetime
- The decision to move anywhere that didn't work out
- That time we said the wrong thing
- The time we didn't say anything when we should have spoken up

The list could go on, beautiful someone. Make your own and give it a sledgehammer slam, then sweep the dust off a cliff somewhere, or burn it, anything that tells your heart and your soul that these memories no longer have a hold on you. You can move on without them, stepping out into your future with courage, unencumbered by the fears and hesitations these memories always evoked in you.

They are gone. We are done with them. They were yesterday's story. We're writing a new one now.

And we *exhale*.

## "Choose another thought"

This thing. This *thing* I was losing sleep over. A really smart friend suggested that I just "choose another thought." Huh. Choose another thought. *Choose another thought?*

Me: "Oh please. It can't be that simple."

"Yes," she said, "it *is* that simple. More to the point, it's the only solution. No one can come into your mind and erase the programming that's making you loop on the problem over and over. There's medication for that, but with side effects. Or you can consciously, on purpose, deliberately choose another thought."

Annoying in a way, but also true.

When negative memories start to crop up, when I'm ready to slap myself with a destructive label (for me those would be things like *untalented, unworthy,* and *waaaay too emotional*), I know now that I just can't allow myself to jump down those rabbit holes. I literally can't afford it if I want to write and draw and publish and create for us, beautiful someone. I can't afford to focus on the chip in my tooth and miss everything else about me that is decent and good and honest and loving and hardworking. I owe it to everyone and everything I care about not to tunnel down into these bottomless pits because if I do, I will never be able to share my very best and fulfill the purpose that has been put in my heart and brain and hands.

Zoom out, and we can see that it's *our responsibility* to use the incredible superpower between our ears to choose good thoughts and discard bad ones, even if that requires daily effort. To ingrain this positive habit, we may need to take ourselves aside for a good talking-to on a regular basis, like this:

- "No, I am not going to re-live that. I learned everything I could from it, and even if I didn't, it's ancient history."
- "I was so young. I know better now."
- "My intentions were loving, even though it didn't work out. And I apologized."
- "I can't do anything to change what happened. Yes, it hurt, but my life since then is testimony to my recovery."
- "I tried it; it didn't work. I moved on."
- "Yes, it hurt me and made me think less of myself, but I've taken over that space in my brain. No one's going to make me feel bad about my body again."
- "I got angry. It wasn't my proudest moment — but I'm human. And I set up an important boundary, even if it was a little sloppy in the making."

...and then, we reinvent the moment, that memory — *that* one — that shot into our consciousness. We take a deep breath, put a hand over our heart, and say, out loud if we can, a thought-shifting positive affirmation:

- "I am strong."
- "I am beautiful."
- "I am confident."
- "I am good."

- "I am worthy."
- "I am calm."
- "I am focused."
- "I am capable."
- "I am loved."
- "I am loving."
- "I am kind."
- "I am generous."
- "I am blessed."
- "I am enough."

We make a cup of tea, FaceTime a loving friend, listen to a favorite track, go to the easel/loom/garden/workshop/yoga mat or someplace else that we find safe and welcoming.

Wait, what bad memory?

## What matters

*I think it's brave that you get up in the morning even if your soul is weary. I think it's brave that you keep on living even if you don't know how to anymore. I know there are days when you feel like giving up, But I think it's brave that you never do.*

— Lana Rafaela

What are we *braving* exactly? We are braving ourselves. More specifically, *being* ourselves. The honest-to-goodness unique core of who we really are.

That has to start with knowing ourselves well enough to speak out. To love what we love. To pursue goals that are meaningful to us. To ask the questions we need answered. To persist when we're being told to sit down and be quiet. To stand our ground when we're being embarrassed into thinking we're the only one who ever asked that question/objected to the abuse/doesn't understand. To go against the crowd, heck to walk directly through it to the other side, biffed and boffed and buffeted, against the tide. To ask, as one professional woman did, "What if I don't want any more success? What if this is enough? Is that okay?" (Why does she even have to ask?)

Knowing ourselves doesn't mean we sit-around-and-navel-gaze in self-absorption. It just means we take the time to lift our heads up from getting the kids and finding a dentist and asking for a raise and calling the insurance company. To pause between wondering if we're getting enough Vitamin D and whether that's an actual wrinkle and how much it really matters that the price of tomatoes went up.

When we drop every preoccupation and distraction, strip everything else away (every attachment, every possession, our current situation...) our true priorities and passions are what's left.

Knowing what these are can come gently from years of experience and more abruptly from "Aha!" experiences too. In most of our lives, it'll be a combination.

So what are they?

## Grace, gratitude, generosity, and grit

My monitor is covered with sticky notes, all sizes and colors. I'm a jotter. To-dos, quotes, reminders, I've got 'em everywhere. Right now I'm looking at a yellow sticky that says: "grace, gratitude, generosity, and grit."

It was part of an effort to simplify the branding of Blossie's Books, messaging I've been working on for the last five years. I've had that sticky up for a while now because these four words are a great summary not only of what Blossie's Books are about, but also what makes life truly meaningful to me (<u>not</u> co-incidentally the same thing ☺).

**Grace:** This one I also have inked on my right wrist next to a ruby-throated hummingbird. This is grace under pressure, under fire (which we so often are). It is being forgiving in the real sense of the meaning of the word which is to give again as before, as if the offense never happened (definitely not always there yet, but at least always trying to be!). It is honoring my history by acting my age and not reverting back to childish behaviors and reactions. It's owning my power, the full breadth and depth of it and having the courage to be strong and outspoken in tough situations because as a human being, I have the right and the responsibility to do that.

**Gratitude:** If you know me, beautiful someone, you already know how I feel about the importance of gratitude. In one way or another, I've included it in literally every book I've ever written and dedicated full sections of *Dream Come True* and *The Becoming Journal* to it. Gratitude softens us by ensuring that we don't feel entitled. One of the best definitions of gratitude I ever heard was from my friend Gracie who said, "Gratitude makes me see that what I have is enough. I don't need to grab for more." It shows other people that we are thankful for their help, their support, their example, their love. Gratitude is a pause, a breath we take that stops the grasping and striving in our lives long enough for us to acknowledge and savor everything we've already received. And in all these ways, gratitude is a spiritual multivitamin.

**Generosity**: If gratitude is a multivitamin, then generosity is a yoga and meditation practice. Generosity includes giving in all its forms, certainly material things, but also giving of our time, sharing our gifts with other people, connecting people with each other, making the effort to smile or compliment someone who seems to need it, even when we really don't feel like doing it. Generosity opens a flow that travels in both directions: out from us and also back toward us. It relaxes us physically by loosening our grip on our stuff and eventually opening our hands on everything we have so we can share it and in so doing, multiply it.

**Grit**: "Fall down seven times, get up eight" is a Japanese proverb. Brilliance in seven words. Because beautiful someone, we must. We have no choice. If we are alive, we will fall down again (and again) and need to get up again (and again — and again). Some of this is perseverance and determination, both of which empower us to keep on pushing forward, no matter what. But *grit*...grit is what we use to stand back up again, refusing to be a victim. Grit means we accept our profound responsibility to ourselves and the people we care about. It's what we use to get up after we're knocked down by a job loss, bad relationship, rejection letter, financial spasm. Not only do we get up again, we come up *swinging* — whatever that means in the moment. We take the hit, mourn for a little while, but then we stand up, dust ourselves off, and start job networking, make a clean break from the relationship, submit our work to another publisher/agent/gallery/prospect and then 20 more, face the financial music by creating a bill payment and savings plan (even if that means putting aside just $5 a week...guess how I know this? ☺).

For sure, my list will keep evolving, but I think it's a good summary of my passions — the intangibles that matter to me so very much, my guiding principles. The qualities that add spiritual structure and meaning to my life.

Elsewhere in my sticky note montage as well as in the handwritten journals I have strewn on the floor of my closet, in my drawers, and on my bookshelves are the lessons that I've learned in time. If I pan out for the hope-addicted, joy-sustaining big picture and challenge myself to summarize these, here's what I have (so far):

*What really matters to me*
- Lasting joy not temporary happiness
- Time not money
- Relationships not acquaintances
- People not stuff
- Health not appearance
- Personal pride not public recognition
- Cooperating not competing
- Understanding not winning
- Joyful work not money

*What I know for sure*
- There is no cosmic notebook with all our mistakes written in it that we have to pay for. Translation: we don't deserve bad things when they happen.
- We deserve whatever we're willing to work for.
- When we're wrong and we apologize sincerely, it's over. Guilt has no place in a healthy and authentic life.

- When someone takes something the wrong way, we are not responsible. We can still apologize if we hurt them, but we know in our own hearts what our intentions were, and those intentions matter.
- We don't have to do things that make us feel icky in order to be acceptable.
- Our choices are ours. They are not right. They are not wrong. They are ours.
- Our uniqueness is not wrong; it's well, *unique*. Different.
- The future is unwritten. It is not predetermined by fate, genetics, history, expectations, or what other people have done. It is ours to create.

Maybe most of all, I am always hopeful; I believe it's worth striving, maybe even fighting for happiness and joy and peace because they are possible, regardless of circumstances. Not always right away, and sometimes only after a long fight back to the surface, but possible, yes.

I have a natural optimism, and no matter what happens, I have this persistent belief that it's possible to be joyful at any point. I'm *completely unimpressed* by status, believe love is better than any possession, think the story of a family struggling on a store manager's income is far more heroic and interesting than the expensive toys and trappings of a wealthy investment banker. I deeply believe in living honestly and think that honesty is the greatest of freedoms. Confidence in myself is so much better than the admiration of others. I believe humility and empathy are the two most important and attractive qualities in a human being. And I know that if I want to be loved, I must be loving. If I want to receive, I must be giving without expectation or ego.

If I don't write, I get intellectually depressed. If I don't weave, I get creatively depressed. If I don't dig in the dirt, my hands start to itch.

What else? Oh—if eat gluten, I feel sick for days. I can't grow raspberries in my garden, but wild blackberries grow like weeds and taste much better with no effort! Life is short. Fear of failure is a ridiculous motivator. No matter how bad Winter is, Spring always comes, and it is gloriously beautiful. The scent of pine needles warmed by the sun mixed with sea spray on Cape Cod, Massachusetts is like nothing else on Earth.

## Okay beautiful, your turn

Make a cup of something yummy, grab a pencil and some paper, and most of all, a quiet place and think along these lines:

- What really matters to you?
- Who matters?
- What would you not want to live without?
- What do you hope for?
- What makes your life feel complete and right?
- What job or project or get-together causes you to wake up the morning of without an alarm clock?
- What makes you jump out of the shower searching for your phone to record an idea you just had?

Maybe dig a little deeper for some self-reflection:

- What have you changed your mind about in the last five years?
- What do you do when you're nervous?
- Where and when do you feel most at home?

- What makes you laugh?
- If you were to start a business, what would it be?
- If you were to go back to work for someone else, what type of company would you choose?
- If you could go back to school, what would you study?
- What are the five best things that have happened in your life?
- What's the greatest discovery you made about your life in the last five years?
- What kind of day do you look forward to most?
- When have you stood up for yourself?
- When have you stood up for someone else?
- If you were writing a letter to your teenage self, what would the first sentence be?

Scribble, draw, doodle, write actual sentences. All this is for your eyes only, so give yourself the freedom and space to be completely honest.

Then, take a break and come back to read what you wrote. What picture of your true authentic self emerges? I'm gonna bet there are some surprises (these always come when we allow ourselves the time and space to be quiet and think for ourselves), some smiles, some frustration too. It's all in there, right?

Here's the thing, and this part's for all the marbles, beautiful someone: we owe this person, this picture that takes shape in our notebooks when we are at our most honest and sincere — our authentic selves — to the world. Thanks to our total uniqueness, literally no one else can do exactly what we can, the way we can. No one else can create what we can. No one else can solve what we can. No one else can love the way we can.

It's our highest purpose to let this person live and breathe and love and give to the world. Ultimately, braving it is both a peaceful, spiritual way to live and an absolute responsibility to ourselves and the people we love and influence.

# Part 2: Coming home

"We shall not cease
from exploration
And the end of
all our exploring
Will be to arrive
where we started
And know the place
for the first time."

– T.S. Eliot
from "Little Gidding"
*Four Quartets*

DIANA DAVIN

It's time beautiful someone, for us to come home to ourselves, where we can relax. Kick off our shoes, throw on our sweats and comfy T-shirt, the one with the holes and faded logo. Turn off the phone. Shut the laptop. Stop looking right and left for cues and rules about how we're supposed to act, what we're supposed to say, who we're supposed to be.

It's time to go where our brave hearts are safe, where we don't have to worry about doing the right thing or making sure everyone is comfortable with us. Where we can finally lose the idea that somehow we have to prevent the world from knowing who we truly are.

We can do all this, and here we will...

**Relax into honesty**
**Brave your boundaries**
**Own your amazing**
**Find (or create) work you love**
**Bless this body**
**Let only love in**
**Stop explaining!**
**Shhh...listen!**
**Face it**
**Create your joy**

DIANA DAVIN

## Relax into honesty

I have insecurities of course,
but I don't hang out with anyone
who points them out to me.

— Adele

In yoga there is a concept called *satya*, a Sanskrit word that means truthfulness. It refers to a virtue in our thoughts and words that once developed, prevents us from distorting the truth. We are honest and real in what we think, say, and do. When this ideal is reached, when truth emanates from each of us, the world is in balance: it makes sense, holds together, and works harmoniously.

Of course, the opposite is also true: without this essential truth in each of our lives, we splinter and break apart. Our lives are out of balance and by extension, the world doesn't make sense or work right.

I've discovered *satya* recently and along with the other yamas in the Yoga Sutra — ahimsa (non-violence), asteya (non-stealing), aparigraha (non-possessiveness), and brahmacharya (fidelity) — and begun to feel drawn to these ideas because of their simplicity and because they welcome everyone. There's no sense of you're in, but you're out; you believe what we believe so you're part of the club, you don't ask too many questions, you say the right things (whatever that means).

I like that, beautiful someone. It's a kind of Utopia as far as I'm concerned. A place where everyone is honest and real. Everyone is welcomed and accepted.

All because of something so simple that's completely in our power to do: *be true*.

Our journey to brave starts with our willingness to tell the truth. To be honest about everything in and around us. The truth about who we are, what we love, our boundaries, our passions and our values. If we aren't being honest in these ways, we're we can't possibly live bravely.

We can start by acknowledging and respecting our own truths. This can't help but radiate out from us to the world around us. Essentially, when we're true to ourselves, we can't be fake to others. That's my clumsy paraphrase of Shakespeare in the scene from *Hamlet* where Polonius gives his son advice about how to be in the world:

> *This above all: to thine own self be true,*
> *And it must follow, as the night the day,*
> *Thou canst not then be false to any man.*

In some ways, telling the truth is just that simple: being true to ourselves.

In some ways, it's not.

Our lives, our families, our friendships, our work, our communities…are all complex. Society has rules and expectations of us. We are under any number of pressures to fit in: make an appearance at the right time, say the right thing, avoid saying the wrong thing, and in general be a decent human being. That all requires judgment, timing, choice, intuition, and quite often courage.

## With love

Do you know someone who takes pride in saying, "You always know exactly where you stand with me; I'm very blunt"? This honesty run amok is an attempt to reframe laziness and bad manners into virtues! Blunt people are often poor listeners who are more concerned about what they want to say than what other people need to hear (or avoid hearing). They leave lots of hurt feelings in their wake...and that's definitely not a virtue.

Being truthful doesn't mean saying everything we think or verbalizing every emotion we experience. Sometimes taking care with our delivery of the truth by finding the right time, the right tone, and the right words to be honest with someone is the best thing to do.

Sometimes the truth comes after we validate someone's feelings ("I understand how you feel," "I was in a situation like that once and I reacted the same way," "After everything that you've gone through in the last few months, it's no wonder you'd react that way"). Sometimes sheer compassion moves us to choose love as truth and say something kind, especially about a feature, idea, or choice someone has made, regardless of what the blunt reality might be ("I think your hair looks great!" "The pants are beautiful, and you look gorgeous," "Whatever you decided to say in that moment was right — you're not the type of person to fly off the handle" "I'm sure you're the best person for the job; you've worked so hard").

In his letter to the Ephesians, the Christian Apostle Paul wrote about the importance of speaking the truth in love, approaching someone and talking to them with an attitude of love. That means that the motive of the entire conversation, whatever the subject, is love, not bluntness or superiority and not a correction that does more harm than good. An attitude of love is one of helping the person we're talking to, deciding that anything less will not be constructive.

Sometimes *silence* is speaking the truth in love, like when we have nothing helpful to say and we know it. Love and kindness put the brakes on verbalizing thoughts that are honest but might hurt. We measure our words carefully and say very little (if anything) in order to be gentle with someone who's suffering.

## Relaxing into honesty

I know that I have sometimes deliberately and sometimes unconsciously moved away from situations (jobs, friendships, romances, opportunities, social events) in which I could not be honest. I find it totally exhausting to be fake. And there is something (maybe writing this will even help me figure out exactly what it is) that I find absolutely stomach-turning about phoniness.

Maybe it's that I spent a lot of my life surrounded by people who always had an agenda, and I was (and am) a what-you-see-is-what-you-get person. I was always slow to get the joke. Innocent in the face of sarcasm and insults. The too serious person in the room, the one who's easy to take advantage of. Subtlety and indirection, especially when they're being used to settle a score, are often lost on me.

Three years had passed since I ran a communications workshop for leaders in the fashion industry. *Three years.* I was in a T.J. Maxx flipping through the leggings rack when all of a sudden I looked up and thought, "Ohhhh! *That's* why she left!"

The head of the team had ducked out early after the workshop without a "Thanks" or "Talk soon." It was there, surrounded by leggings at T.J. Maxx that it dawned on my sometimes glacially slow brain that she left because she was mad. At me. During the workshop, I'd given her archrival the floor on a sensitive topic, and in doing so, undermined her authority. My mind zipped back to that day, the look on her face, her attitude toward me during the break, and of course, her early exit.

I got it, but it took me *three years*.

I don't always get the indirection, in this case, the meaning of the brush off. My brain screams, "Just say what you're thinking so we can deal with it! Don't make me guess!!" It takes so much energy to deal with subtle digs and indirection: we have to remember who we're "supposed to" be in a given situation, how we're "supposed to" react, who we're "supposed to" be mad at, instead of just reacting naturally out of who we truly are, reactions that are as organic as jumping at a noise, laughing at a joke, smiling at a baby, reaching for the warmth and softness of a dog who wants to cuddle.

When we are honest, we are at peace, with nothing to prove, and nothing to fake. We don't have to waste our energy trying to figure out what someone means when they're being deliberately vague. No need to take part in conjecture or gossip or chameleon ourselves to fit in. We're surrounded by people who truly love *us*, the real thing, not some ersatz version of ourselves manufactured to persuade them that we're worth loving.

We can relax. And as we relax into honesty, as a bonus, we end up with lots more time and energy. Honesty is just a whole lot less work: less calculating, less worrying, and no mental gymnastics. I am convinced down to my bones that living this way adds a decade to our lives.

| Relaxing into honesty means... | ...and can sound like: |
|---|---|
| *Being honest about what we want* | • "Thanks, but I'd rather..."<br>• "I'd like to try..."<br>• "I'm interested in..." |
| *Being clear about what we will and won't do* | • "I'd rather not."<br>• "That's not my thing..."<br>• "Thanks, but I can't make that a priority right now."<br>• "I can't help, but let me tell you what I *can* do..." |
| *Being open about what we like and don't like* | • "Actually, I *didn't* enjoy..."<br>• "Not really..."<br>• "I actually *would* like to try that..." |
| *Being okay with being different from the crowd* | • "I actually disagree."<br>• "I'd rather..."<br>• "I prefer..."<br>• "We're all individuals..." |
| *Being honest about what we think and believe* | • "In my experience..."<br>• "I believe..."<br>• "I think..."<br>• "It's always clear to me that..." |
| *Apologizing when we should* | • "I didn't realize..."<br>• "I'm so sorry..." |
| *Trusting our guts when something doesn't feel right and saying so* | • "That doesn't align with the facts."<br>• "It didn't happen that way..."<br>• "Actually, that doesn't answer my question. I wanted to know if..." |

| | |
|---|---|
| *Telling someone when they hurt us* | - "I was hurt by that…"<br>- "It wasn't funny to me."<br>- "Wow, that hurts my feelings!" |
| *Leaving a conversation having been true to our standards* | - "I deeply believe…"<br>- "I disagree that…"<br>- "That's not something I'd do…"<br>- "I think we need to agree to disagree on this." |
| *Enforcing our boundaries* | - "Please respect my decision."<br>- "That's my choice."<br>- "That's private."<br>- "I don't talk about that."<br>- "I can stay for an hour." |

DIANA DAVIN

*BRAVING IT*

# Brave your boundaries

Don't you ever let a soul in the world tell you that you can't be exactly who you are.

— Lady Gaga

"*I have never felt the need for privacy more than I did after all those months of quarantine. Being together with my husband and our kids in the house takes its toll. I'm a homebody, so it wasn't being home that was making me crazy; it was the complete lack of privacy. My husband saw what I had for breakfast, lunch, and dinner. He knew when I was going out to buy dental floss. He knew what time I woke up and how many cups of coffee I drank and how many hours I worked and who I called. And I knew all this about him. The togetherness with the kids was great at times and especially in the beginning, but after a while I was going out of my mind. And the part that was really hard: I felt like I had no personal space."*

–Alexa

No matter who we are close to and who we are not, whether we are more comfortable alone or surrounded by people, we really are *individuals*. In some ways, the need for personal sovereignty, the freedom to make our choices without having to announce or explain them, is hard-wired into each of us. And honoring this need with courage and authenticity is as organic to our brave as breathing.

This is why what Alexa said made so much sense. No one wants every aspect of their lives open and visible, not even to the people they're closest to. We all need private time. We need space. Specifically, we need our *own* space.

And that, beautiful someone, means *boundaries.*

## *The Gift of No*

Boundaries are the lines where other people end and we begin. They are the spaces and places inside ourselves that are private and inviolable. And when we choose to live our lives courageously, they are lines *we* define and *we* protect as if our authentic lives depend on it...because they do. Our choices in this regard are nonnegotiable.

Boundaries are so important to our happy/healthy/sane that I dedicated an entire book to this topic in *The Gift of No*, a book whose tagline says it all: "*Stop saying yes when you really mean no and start taking better care of yourself and the people you love!*"

Boundaries let us take care of ourselves and the people we love, while they embolden our souls by keeping them safe from harm. They help shield us from crazy makers: people, activities, situations, jobs, relationships, and projects that are just wrong for us. And while we may *choose* to build our own strength and resilience by spending time with challenging people in situations that stretch us, the key is we're *choosing* to do so. We don't allow boundary-crashing crazy-makers to push us into painful situations that drag us down.

Boundaries are our no-zones, as I called them in *The Gift of No*. They are fundamental to our happy/healthy/sane and our courageous and authentic lives. (Beautiful someone, if you haven't already done so, my heart to yours, I would strongly encourage you to grab a copy of *The Gift of No*. You can literally read it in an afternoon, and it's filled with ideas for knowing your own unique boundaries and making them stick in a host of different situations.)

Without boundaries, our choices are not our own. We pick our heads up and find ourselves in situations and with people we never would have chosen. We've just been pulled and pushed, our preferences and goals ignored, our boundaries wide open and completely fungible. It's impossible to live true to our own lives and plans unless we know what our boundaries are, how to set them up and protect them.

In *The Gift of No*, true to its title, I explored the power of the word "no" to draw lines around our time and choices in ways that define our personal space and individuality. I'm including a key section here as a reminder of how to define our boundaries on our way to living as the bold and brave individuals we are!

### Find your need for no

Your no-zones are unique. They outline a personal space that no one gets to invade without your permission. They are boundary lines where other people end and you—one-of-a-kind, matchless, personal you—begin.

Some examples of no-zones, obvious and maybe not-so-obvious:

- Your privacy
- Any subject you don't want to talk about
- Standards on which you don't compromise

- Your choices (about life, career, your future, relationships...pretty much anything)
- How people speak to you and treat you
- How you spend your time
- Your relationship with your significant other
- Your relationships with the other important people and loves of your life (kids, parents, siblings, friends...)
- Your weight, haircut, clothes, or any other aspect of your physical appearance
- Your diet or eating habits
- Your finances
- Exercise: how often, how much, the kind of exercise you do and where you do it (this includes the decision NOT to make exercise a part of your life)
- Your political views
- Your faith/spiritual beliefs
- Your history or heritage
- Where you go for the holidays

There are lots more, but here's the key point: YOU draw your no-zones, and that means YOU get to decide where they are. It also means that only you get to make exceptions and move them temporarily if and when you choose to, and only you get to redraw them if and when you want to (for example, in a specific situation or relationship or when you want someone's advice). It also means you decide whose opinions about your no-zones you choose to value and listen to, and whose you don't.

Again, this doesn't mean we shouldn't challenge ourselves and sometimes update our thinking. It's important to consider good information from people we trust, stories posted by well-sourced news outlets worthy of our attention, empirical evidence on trends that may change how we feel about an important topic, etc. All of this is part of being healthy and open-minded and evolving as a person.

Having boundaries just means that we are careful about the quality of information that we absorb and that we are sure to process it *ourselves* into choices that make sense for *us*. This is vastly different from zig-zagging everywhere in reaction to the ideas and opinions and experiences that we read or hear about.

As we brave our lives, we take in good information, and then *we make our own decisions.*

## Our journey into brave

For all these reasons, I thought we should absolutely include in our journey into *Braving It* the critical role that strong, healthy boundaries play in a courageous life. Because when we are living boldly, we are living by our own goals and dreams and values and not fearfully walking around absorbing information from any and every source as if it were the law or cosmic guidance on how "good" people live their lives.

Back to *The Gift of No*:

> So now: where are your unique no-zones? Try thinking about them in two ways: what you want in your life, and what you don't.
>
> **What you want**
> By "what you want" I mean who and what matters to you, where you want your life to go. (If this sounds like setting up your goals and priorities, that's not a coincidence!) What does this have to do with your no-zones? An awful lot, it turns out.

Clear priorities outline what's important to you. Without them, it's harder to say no and enforce other boundaries. Some examples:

Instead of deliberately going after a relationship she knows would be right for her, Sam gets involved in the one that lands in her lap, and it's kind of, you know, okay. Whenever she sees other couples who are deliriously happy though, she gets a little queasy.

Instead of actively, on purpose creating the circumstances that will move him toward his dreams, Justin just sits back to "wait and see" and then reacts to whatever happens. So even though he desperately wants to live in SoCal, he doesn't set up his life to be ready if the chance comes up. When the opportunity actually arises, he doesn't have the money or job flexibility to make the move.

Instead of making decisions based on her plans and ambitions, Claire makes choices based on how she feels on a given day. So even though she always wanted to write music, she never felt like putting together a plan for making it happen. All her random notes and ideas sit on sheets of paper in her sock drawer, and she just feels bad every time she walks by her dresser. "Bucket list," she thinks, but then, "if ever."

Again, without clear goals and strong ideas about what really matters to you, it's harder to say no and enforce other boundaries. So you hear yourself saying things like, "Yeah, sure. Count me in. I don't have any other plans" and "Okay, I'll do it. I've got nothing to lose." Can you hear how easy it is—when you don't have goals—to get knocked off course by a boundary blaster or end up running around aimlessly after everyone's random demands on your time?

On the other hand, when you know your goals, your no-zones are strong, and you say things like: "You know, that's not the best use of my time right now" or "I'm close to finally launching my new business. If I say yes to this, I'm gonna lose momentum it's taken six months to build. No can do."

**So how do you want to spend your time?**
When you're serious about your goals, you can prioritize your time and organize your life. And if something—anything—gets in the way, maybe by making demands on your time that zap your energy so you can't work your plan, you automatically know that thing is hitting a no-zone for you.

Every day has basically a 16-hour budget of awake time. What do you want to spend it on?

- Raising amazing, self-sufficient, happy kids
- Staying healthy and fit
- Helping other people stay healthy and fit
- Writing novels or short stories
- Writing nonfiction books in your area of expertise
- Climbing the corporate ladder
- Building your ad agency
- Spending time with your partner
- Renovating your apartment
- Earning a PhD in math
- Teaching high school science
- Counseling at-risk kids
- Conserving natural resources

- Working in animal rescue

Make a list of how you want to spend your time, and then take an honest look at how you <u>are</u> spending it. Are you living by your priorities or blowing whichever way the wind takes you, for example:

- Does your life, the way it's set up now, reflect your goals and priorities? Is your time devoted to the people, goals, and activities that really matter to you?
- Do you take conscious awake time to think about your goals and reset them as your life changes?
- Do the important people in your life know your plans and priorities?
- Are you aware of obstacles to living your life according to your priorities? Are you working on moving those obstacles out of the way?

This can be a real wake-up call if you haven't given it any thought...or much thought lately. But driven, focused, successful (and soon-to-be successful!) people live with their goals and priorities top of mind. They have the courage to say a firm and clear no to obstacles that show up as no-zone crashers and boundary blasters making demands on their time that would require them to take a detour away from what matters most to them.

**Your have-to-haves**

And while we're on the topic of what you want, let's talk about your have-to-haves. What do you absolutely have to have in your life to feel happy, healthy, and sane?

- Work/life balance

- Good friends
- Challenging work or projects
- A predictable schedule
- Spontaneity!
- Creative outlets
- Solitude

How about at work? Real answers from real people:

- "I need to be able to leave at 5:00 without having anyone judge and give me the stare."
- "I have to completely trust the people I work with."
- "I really like spending time with coworkers outside the office. It helps me see people as humans and helps me work with them better."
- "I need predictable routine."
- "I can't stand routine—give me a variety of assignments and challenges or I will shrivel up and die!"

**Up next: what you don't want**
Whether they're doing it consciously or not, who are the space invaders in your life: (love-her-forever-but) Mom? Manager? In-law? Neighbor? Friend? Second cousin? Client? Customer?

What kinds of things do they ask you to do?

When do they ask—can you predict it, e.g., holidays, vacations, busy seasons at work...? Or maybe the boundary crashing isn't predictable: you get cornered at a party or texted in the middle of the work day or at the last minute when you're too busy to think straight about what you're agreeing to. Your space invaders may play on your sympathies or loyalties or history—or all three: "Your help always means so much to the kids, and it's great that I can always count on you. If you don't say yes, the kids will miss out this year!"

What do your space invaders assume about your time and ability to help them, for instance if you're stay-at-home or self-employed (or both), do they think you can drop everything to help them because you have "nothing else to do" or unlimited time or complete control over your time?

How about prying: what do they want to know that you just don't want to spill?

What about their expectations based on your talents: you can bake an amazing cake, meet "impossible" deadlines, organize anything, schedule like you're planning a royal wedding, lift furniture like the Hulk?

Are there people in your life who take advantage of these talents, even using flattery to persuade you:

- "Your cakes are a work of art. I would love to have everyone at the party see one. It would be the centerpiece of the dessert table!"
- "I wouldn't think about moving that antique armoire without you!"
- "You're my go-to person for this kind of assignment. No one but you could even come close to getting this done on time. You can make time for it, I'm sure."

Too much?

Keep it simple then: what's on your "never again" list? Maybe it's sitting in six hours of holiday traffic on the way to not-your-favorite cousin's house, or watching your neighbor's kids for two hours longer than you agreed to because she got "tied up" at an appointment—again.

What situations or circumstances make you crazy uncomfortable, like maybe a not-too-close friend's constant griping about EVERYTHING or standing around with nothing to say at your college roommate's annual New Year's party?

What demands on your time and talents give you the feeling that someone else's needs always matter more than yours? Who's making those demands?

When do you feel that you're compromising in an area that for you is non-negotiable, stuff of the "don't even go there with me" variety, like:

- "I won't talk about [*that subject*]."
- "I never skip time with my [*Mom/ Dad/ brother/sister/kids/Great Aunt Tillie...whoever*]."
- "I will not cancel plans I've made with my family."
- "If I say I'll be there, I'll be there. I'd have to lose a leg to ditch on a commitment I've made."

What are your non-negotiables in relationships?

- "Don't mess with my friends."
- "I need my space."
- "Loyalty is everything to me."

- "If someone stretches the truth with me, I cannot trust them again."
- "If he/she cheats, we're done."

The prompts you need to pinpoint your no-zones would fill a whole book, but you get the idea.

Think about your lists of what you want and don't want in your life. All your must-haves and hot buttons are telling a story: the situations, people, behaviors, demands, standards, and circumstances you want in your life, and just as important, the ones you don't.

And even if nothing on your lists is a major surprise to you, thinking about all this might help you understand yourself a little better ("Oooh, yeah, that must be why I cringe every time her number comes up on my phone!" or "Now I totally get why I was so unhappy at that job! It pushed every button I have!")

**That feeling you get**
Still too much? Okay, skip the lists. You're not that type. You can still tell where your no-zones are by that twisting, icky feeling you get when someone's getting close to one. Please respect that feeling when it hits you! Realize it means the person is headed straight for a boundary that matters to you. Make a mental note of the person, the circumstances, the request and the timing. Be sure you avoid that combo in the future.

A note here though, beautiful someone: those of us with no-zone issues often have a chronic case of gut distrust. We know based on gut feeling that we shouldn't be doing something (think handing that item to the cashier knowing it's an expensive mistake, clicking on that link that's going to suck an hour of time that could be spent in much better ways, reaching for that second or third or fifth slice of anything...) but we do it anyway! Or we know when something just doesn't feel right (the commission-only job offer, the date with someone's second cousin who's been living in his parents' basement "temporarily" for the last year, the investment we don't really understand but the broker is making sound like such a sure thing), but we do it anyway!

How 'bout let's not, and instead start to trust that gut feeling that always seems to be spot-on in hindsight.

# DIANA DAVIN

# Own your amazing

> I worshipped dead men for their strength, forgetting I was strong.
>
> — Vita Sackville-West

Gina had made a lemon cake, with white frosting and lemon slices carefully arranged around the top and sides. There were decorations in the icing that mixed the cloud-white frosting with the softest yellow puffs and gorgeous detail piped into the icing up and down all seven layers.

The cake was beautiful, not just because it was decorated so intricately, but because of how Gina talked about it, and how she had stayed up until 2 AM making it. "I just forget about everything when I'm baking," she said. "It's like meditation to me, and I really love the final product when it's done!"

Which was so great to hear, especially knowing that Gina was going through some very tough days having lost her father, and then less than a year later, her mother to cancer. I put an arm around her shoulder, and she leaned into the hug. But then, she started to take the very gift we were looking at and put it down: "I know it's not perfect, I mean the lemon slices are uneven and if you look on the side the decorations really look kind of globby. I tried my best but, well, this is all I could come up with."

My heart broke for her, not just because of the obvious having lost both parents inside of a year, but because she was taking her beautiful gift of creativity that brought her so much joy and peace and putting it down.

We *all* do this — not sure why exactly — but we all do it. Somehow, we manage to take one of our unique and precious superpowers, whatever it is, and denigrate it, making it not as good as: other people, experts, we could be, we should be at this point, pictures online...

Dahlias are my friend Pete's pride and joy. Get him talking about his dahlias, and you'll literally be backed into a corner for at least an hour (guess how I know this... ☺). And even though I tease him, Pete is a joy. When he starts talking about the proliferation of dahlias in his garden and seeds versus bulbs and heirloom varieties and colors and how to dig up and store the bulbs in the winter and how the bulbs spread and the unbelievable variety of sizes and colors, and after *ooing* and *ahing* as he scrolls through picture after picture, it's exhausting but, in its own way, electric.

Yet every conversation also includes lots of personal criticism: how he could do better and how he wishes he'd started sooner and he doesn't know anywhere near as much as he should and last year's garden was a fail...

This is it, beautiful someone. This is what we do...our collective burden of perfectionism. I blogged about this...

> "Hey, I'm not perfect," my friend Gia likes to say. "I've got this little chip in my tooth right here."

LOL, but seriously, aren't we all a little like this: always pushing ourselves, expecting perfection? And when we don't get it (it's easy to find a tiny "chip" in even our greatest victories), we're so busy stressing over the small imperfection that we forget to celebrate the success.

> Or we think that ignoring our successes and sprinting ahead to the next challenge makes us more "serious" about our goals.
>
> Or we're too worried about losing our edge to stop and give ourselves a well-deserved pat on the back.
>
> Or we just don't want to let ourselves believe we're "good enough."

In *Dream Come True*, I wrote about something I call The Comparison Game, the incredible burden of comparing ourselves to other people:

> We spend waaay too much time looking at everyone else, reading about "overnight" successes (who have almost always worked 10 years behind the scenes be-fore getting their big break), about prodigies and instant billionaires.
>
> Then, after packing all this into our brains and hearts, we innocently take a look in the mirror and see...what exactly? Truth. Ourselves. Our beautiful, hardworking, honest, naked selves. How—HOW can this compare to the well-written headlines, gorgeous photography, and carefully edited stories showcasing the best of the best and making

dream-reaching look so easy and instant in 100 words or less?

The problem is, we're looking at other people's out-sides with our insides. It's apples and oranges! We're comparing the naked truth about ourselves to other people's made-for-primetime stories! You see? Apples and oranges! Or more like refrigerators and sunscreen: NOTHING in common.

...Here's the truth—and please remember this one down in your beautiful bones—we are different. That's it. That's the reason comparison is such a game in the first place. We are each as unique as our fingerprints, and so comparison, in a very real way, is ridiculous.

...the Comparison Game is a mediocrity magnet that dream seekers have to resist with everything we've got. It is the status quo's most useful weapon, a tiny seed of "You are weird" and "Be ashamed of your out-of-the-box ideas" and "You want to try WHAT?" that takes root if we water it with belief, time, and attention.

Beautiful someone, we're not better or worse than anyone else. We're different from everyone else! This is the real sneaky part of The Comparison Game and a huge way in which it blocks the yes that changes everything. Comparison encourages us to be the same — to ditch the yes that changes everything in favor of the yeses that make us cookie-cutter identical to everyone around us.

*How* can that be good?

If we are creating ourselves by looking at everyone else and making our choices based on theirs, we will all end up looking exactly the same. ("Number 12 Looks Just Like You" is an episode of the original Twilight Zone about this. It's based on "The Beautiful People," a fable by Charles Beaumont about a girl in a futuristic society where everyone has plastic surgery to look identical — seriously creepy, but unforgettable and worth watching!)

And with all this shape-shifting ourselves to be just like everybody else, there's absolutely no room for the yes the changes everything for us and the people we love in our one-of-a-kind lives. We thrive as individuals, as families, as communities, and as a world based on our uniqueness as individuals coming together to create something bigger and better (and definitely more interesting!) as a whole.

Most important of all, we can't ever win The Comparison Game, because in it, we always lose ourselves.

We are unique, we are here once, therefore our unique gift can only be shared within the parenthesis of time that is our lives.

My prayer for us, beautiful someone, is that we realize this, remember it always, and most of all that we run our lives bravely, with a sense of profound responsibility to share our unique and amazing talents with the world.

Our brave souls can celebrate our gifts and achievements, look forward to get better, but also look back at how far we've already come. In the words of author Joyce Meyer, "I'm not yet where I want to be, but thank God I'm not where I used to be. I'm okay, and I'm on my way!"

This way, we're never embarrassed or reluctant to share our gifts, and we definitely never put them down.

## Itchy, sweaty, and red-faced

Full disclosure: I approached writing this section with some trepidation. Self-promotion (and maybe you feel the same way, beautiful someone?) is really uncomfortable for me, like itchy, sweaty, red-faced uncomfortable. So much so that even when I see other people doing it, I cringe and back away. "You're being so obvious! You shouldn't brag on yourself like that!"

In the end though, I realized that I couldn't get away with writing a book about living boldly and courageously without talking about how to brag on our gifts. Or, put another way: I knew I had to have the courage to take on this section as I wrote a book about courage ☺.

Why exactly is being able to talk about our talents in positive ways such an important skill for living boldly and bravely? Interestingly, more for what it says to *us* than what it says to other people.

In psychological terms, bragging is called "self-disclosure," and I was amazed to read about a University of Texas at Austin study that found bragging gives us the same boost in brain chemistry that we get from eating a delicious meal. When study participants bragged about their accomplishments, researchers were able to plot spikes in the brain's meso-limbic dopamine system, the same spikes that occur during happy moments and positive activities. Among their conclusions was the fact that it's actually *healthy* to brag, that bragging somehow talks to *us* as much as it does to other people by letting our own psyches know about our talents and accomplishments and our deserving sense of pride in them.

Backing up even further, when we're able to talk about ourselves in positive ways, we're the first ones to hear it in our own heads. As Ralph Waldo Emerson said, "The ancestor to every action is a thought." The action of positive self-talk begins first with our own healthy and encouraging thoughts about ourselves. Nothing is empowering in quite the same way.

Of course, when we have developed the communication skill to talk about ourselves in positive ways that don't — and this is important — make other people cringe, it changes how they see us and maybe even more important, how they treat us. People are less likely to take liberties, assume we will do things for them without asking, or be demanding or rude with someone they know has healthy self-respect.

## Three groups

When it comes to talking about themselves, people tend to fall into one of three groups: they never talk about themselves, they talk about themselves but just to put themselves down, or they brag so much that everyone around them ends up wilting in discomfort and looking for the exits.

Knowing us, beautiful someone, we fall mostly into the never-talk-about-ourselves group.

*Why* do we do this?

- We tend to err on the side of humility just by nature.
- We're afraid of talking about our success because we worry it won't last.
- We don't make time to acknowledge or celebrate our achievements because we're already sprinting ahead to the next challenge.
- We're naturally generous by nature and would rather cede the limelight to others.
- We never want to be "that guy" (or even close), the one who just won't stop talking about himself.

Years and years (and years) of operating this way have taught me...it's not right or fair to ourselves to not talk about our achievements with confidence in honest, fact-based ways at opportune moments because doing so shows maturity, confidence, and strength of character. Some healthy bragging is an empowering success strategy in life, and certainly at work.

Definitely, our work and accomplishments should be excellent, and stand alone with complete integrity as our best effort — that's a given. And yes, we can sometimes "let our success be our noise." There will be times when working hard in silence is the best brag there is. Sometimes this can be incredibly impactful.

*Sometimes*, but not *all* the time. And maybe more important, mastering this skill shows a level of personal confidence that's attractive to all kinds of good experiences and positive people.

Talking about our achievements and skills isn't inherently boastful. Like anything else, it depends on the delivery and timing. Sometimes sharing information about our achievements and talents can actually help others:

- When people know what we're good at, they know they turn to us for help with that very thing. "You speak fluent Italian? I'm working on a book and one of the scenes I'm writing takes place in an Italian neighborhood in Brooklyn. Maybe you could help me with some of the phrasing?"
- Sharing our skills and accomplishments with other people is a form of closeness to them that may help them feel comfortable doing the same, strengthening the relationship in the process.
- When we show that we're confident, people feel better about connecting with us and involving us in meaningful ways. Their thinking might be something along the lines of, "Well, Jen clearly believes in herself and feels confident about handling this kind of assignment, so I am comfortable trying her out for it."
- When our children hear us talk about ourselves with self-assurance, they understand that confidence is a positive quality, that it's good and right and fundamentally okay for them to genuinely like themselves and feel proud of their achievements and talents.

Beautiful someone, clearly good things can come from talking with other people about the things we excel at. Not only is it okay to share this kind of information about ourselves, it's a bold move that boosts our own confidence and can even help the people around us.

## The art of the brag

There is an art to bragging. It's not just talking about ourselves to anyone who'll listen. The nuances and finer points are essential for ensuring we don't make people squirm with discomfort and look for the exits.

A few ideas to mull over:

- Maybe start by giving yourself a pep talk: "I am proud of my achievements and the skills I've worked so hard to develop. I'm not afraid of my success or what people might expect or think of me once they know what I'm good at."
- As in all our communications, we need to consider the audience. Nothing is worse than walking away from a conversation realizing we made someone uncomfortable by talking about our promotion when they just lost their job or our romantic dinner when they just went through a bad breakup.
- Timing matters too: at a job interview, healthy, balanced bragging is a yes. Coffee with friends when the topic is planning someone's wedding, maybe not so much. The moment is about someone else, and we shouldn't shift the spotlight toward ourselves.
- Be brief. It's best to err on the side of less is more. Don't brag too often and don't go on and on!
- Balance it: brag and humility mix well.
- Stick to the facts. What you accomplished, your proven skills and achievements, things you know you're good at based on feedback you've gotten. (In the words of Mohammad Ali, "It's not bragging if you can back it up.")
- Always mention the people who helped you reach this goal or achieve this end.

- Include and flatter other people who've accomplished what you have, those whose model of success inspired you.

## Flip the script

Have you ever heard someone respond to a genuine compliment with a well-practiced deflection, like this:

*Compliment*: "I love those sandals!"
*Deflection*: "These are so old! I just threw them on because I couldn't find anything else."

*Compliment*: "You did a great job talking to Harry. I think he felt a lot better afterward."
*Deflection*: "Really? I didn't feel like it helped at all!"

*Compliment*: "It's so great that you got into grad school — you must be so excited!"
*Deflection*: "It was really easy to get in. It's actually not a big deal at all, and I'm not even sure I want to go."

Beautiful someone, realize that this does not come across as humble so much as embarrassing for the person who's trying to give us a genuine compliment. It wouldn't be a surprise to find out that the person felt slapped or batted away by these deflections.

Accepting a compliment with confidence and genuine appreciation of someone else is also a form of bragging – and it's a good one. It says that you appreciate that the person noticed your skill or your accomplishment (or your sandals!). It also makes the person delivering the compliment feel good rather than embarrassed.

In a situation where someone is bragging on you with a compliment, even if it makes you uncomfortable, a simple and confident, "Oh, thank you!" is enough.

Other non-deflections:

- "Thanks for mentioning that! I feel really good about it."
- "You're so great! Thanks!"
- "You're right. I forgot about that!"

# Find (or create) work you love

> Work is love made visible.
>
> — Kalil Gibran

**Concept:** You wake up without an alarm, thrilled to jump out of bed and start the day. This is because your work fills you with energy and brings you joy. Sometimes, you're so focused on what you're working on that you literally forget to eat lunch. You work hard all day, and when it's time to wrap up, you feel accomplished and proud, tired but happy. You no longer live for vacations. You enjoy them but are ready to get back to work when they're over.

Mind blow? Maybe, but when we're braving it, we have found or created this kind of work — work we love.

## And yet...

> A businessowner who cares deeply about relationships has alienated many people to build her career, including her partner and her closest friends.

> An MD who went into medicine at her family's urging feels little connection or compassion for her patients.

A lawyer has built a practice that puts such demands on his time that community service and volunteer work — activities that once gave him a great sense of connection and significance — are impossible.

Listen for an important shared characteristic: regardless of their financial success and no matter what business or profession they're in, each of these people is working against one of their most important values or preferences. Chances are they're mostly unaware of the low-grade unhappiness they're feeling beneath the surface of their very busy days. They haven't given all that much thought to what they value or really want out of their work.

And when hands and heart don't match — when we're compromising a standard or ignoring a value that matters to us at work — we're not living honestly.

If independent thinking really matters to us, but we work at a company where initiative is a non-starter,

> If we love to work in a team environment, but spend most of our time at work alone or on a team that's competitive and unsupportive,

> If we do our best work behind the scenes, but are forced to be out in front, visible and put on the spot all the time,

...a low-grade unhappiness eventually morphs into restlessness. Longer term, if nothing changes, it can easily turn into disappointment, resignation, or cynicism about the future and what's possible for us.

## Job joy

For too long (and still), success has been about money, prestige, recognition, benefits, maybe having a corner office. But look at that list again, from money all the way to the corner office: none of those things guarantees happiness. They may bring you joy and if they do, no judgment! But the reality is that there are plenty of people with all of those things who are definitely not happy.

> For many people, it's the purpose of their work that brings them joy. Money and recognition don't matter because their work is meaningful to them, and that's more important than anything.
>
> For others, it doesn't really matter *what* they do, but rather *who* they do it with and for — they'll say that the most important thing for them is the people they work with, the relationships they build through their job.
>
> Other people will say that they really don't want to have a brain-busting job, but rather just want to have fun at work, by doing something light and enjoyable.
>
> Others will say that they really want to work with children or get involved in elder care because this type of work is significant to them based on something that happened in their lives.
>
> Similarly, some people want to work in cancer research or healthcare because they've lost a loved one to a disease and want to give back to the profession that helped that person so much.

Some people are motivated by excitement at work and maybe these people work in sports or entertainment. The excitement in these industries brings them their greatest job joy.

In fact, if you ask a group of people what kind of work makes them happy, you get an incredible range of answers...

- "I have to have new projects, new people, travel...all the time. I can't stand routine!"
- "Hyper-challenge. I like building teams or businesses from scratch, turning bad or even apparently hopeless situations around. But once I get there, I'm itching for the next 'impossible' goal."
- "It doesn't sound ambitious, but I like routine and a predictable schedule in my job. I love knowing exactly what's expected of me...what I have to do to be recognized and succeed."
- "I've got to keep moving. Do not park me behind a desk. And the more time I spend outdoors, the better!"
- "Working with a team that's so tight that we spend time together, even outside of the office."
- "An atmosphere of respect and concern for employees and the customers."
- "A do-or-die goal, especially as I get closer to reaching it."
- "Being able to hang up the phone, knowing I really helped someone is what makes work worthwhile. It sounds corny, but sometimes that actually gives me goosebumps."
- "The freedom of sales. Sales keeps me out in front, not behind the scenes. I would die sitting in an office all day."

Set these comments in a pot and let them simmer. When all else boils away, what's left? For the people who say things like: "I've got to matter to the people I serve" or "I've got to enjoy the people I work with," relationships are paramount. It's as if they're saying, "I do my best when my work relationships are strong."

For people who say, "I need freedom and flexibility" or "I need structure, routine, and predictability," the structure of their days is their principal concern.

People who say things like, "I've got to believe in the company" and "I've got to know the company believes in me" are saying, "The culture and atmosphere of the company I work for really matter to me."

People looking for "hyper-challenge" and exhilarating goals thrive on the thrill of reaching for "impossible" goals.

At the bottom of the pot, we learn that job joy is very personal. The phrase means something different to everyone.

## Courageous choices

My own job joy is driven almost entirely by self-determination and creative contribution, days full of the hard work of making words matter. Spreading hope. Discovering what it means to dream big and then sharing what I've learned about how we can all do that. This required sacrifice, beautiful someone. I closed my consulting practice where I was earning livable revenue and started writing books I had no guarantee anyone would want. I just knew that I had to do this. It didn't matter what it cost me. Consulting brought me no joy, and honestly, a lot of pain (another book for another day...).

A friend who recently graduated college with a degree in Environmental Science decided that her job joy was going to come from making a real difference battling climate change and the many ways in which it affects humanity, from displacement to food insecurity to disease proliferation to maternal and child health issues (all of which are impacted directly and significantly by climate change).

She was offered multiple jobs working for corporations or consulting firms that supported businesses in their efforts to comply with climate regulations and prove that they had done so. But she held out and waited and waited (and waited...) for a position where she'd have a direct, hands-on impact that would change lives for the better — one that was nowhere near as well-paying as those she had been offered. She knew though that money wasn't going to bring her joy; using her knowledge and expertise to help real human beings suffering from the consequences of climate change was.

This is not to be so naïve as to claim that money and benefits aren't important. The parent who is able to comfortably provide for young children by doing a job that may not be exciting or even all that interesting, and may even involve a ton of drudge work, is joyful about being able to pay the bills and take care of their children's futures. The young professional who is able to buy her first apartment and finally achieve financial independence from her parents may find great joy in this meaningful accomplishment, no matter that the job she's doing isn't a thrill a minute for her.

The point is simply this: as we brave our lives, the work we do is chosen for specific reasons that bring us joy. And sometimes we need to make courageous choices in designing our work, choices that enable that work to reflect who we are, what's meaningful to us, and who matters to us.

Those courageous choices may affect where we live, how we live, where we shop, what we can buy, who we work with and for, and of course the type of work we do...all in an effort to live bravely, courageously aligned with the kind of work that brings us joy and enables us to contribute at our highest levels.

My very practical friend Kaitlin used to say that with all the time we spend at work, we should at least enjoy it. "I mean imagine saying that you spend half of your waking time a week at a job that you just hate?" she'd say. "That's a whole lot of time and life energy spent being miserable! Find something you like."

## Now you

What is your job joy? When, where, and how do you do your best work? What gets you so engrossed in your work that you lose track of time?

- The independence of gig work or the structure of 9 to 5?
- Working alone or on a team?
- Managing people or *never* managing people?
- A boss you love so much that you'd run through a wall for them, or any manager will do?
- Constantly changing assignments and goals or predictable work?
- Creative work or research-based projects?
- Customer service or a behind-the-scenes role?
- Helping people or helping a company succeed?

These are just starter thoughts...add your own, but think through what constitutes meaningful work for you, beautiful someone. This is important, and worth spending time on. Once you know, you can make courageous choices about how you spend your precious time and life energy. You may also realize your current work is perfect for you. Either way, you'll discover unexpected energy, unending determination, and the power to persist in your work, regardless of...anything.

## Bless this body

> Mirror, mirror on the wall
> Have I got it?
> Come here, you've always told me
> Who I am.
> I'm finding it's not easy
> To be perfect
> So sorry, you won't define me.
> Sorry, you don't own me.
> Who are you to tell me that I'm less
> than what I should be?
>
> — Barlow Girl
> from their song, *Mirror*

I was 20 once. Then 30 for a while. I'm no longer either of those things.

And I've come to deeply appreciate the fact that one of the greatest beauty secrets is not trying to be something (anything) I'm not. When I tried to look 30 after being 30, I wasn't relaxed, comfortable, or honest.

And I think it showed. As a kind of strain, an unhealthy discomfort, agitation, definitely a lack of confidence.

So today, I'm not 20 or 30. And I realize that I don't want to look like I did then. I want to look like I am now: I've earned these scattered silver hairs, the body changes pregnancy brings, the callouses on my feet from dancing and yoga and the ones on my hands from gardening and weaving. They're all mine. Earned. Acquired at a price. And today, I treasure these badges. I reassure them that they are part of me, they chart me as a map of my history and accomplishments. They trace every step of my life that has led me to where I am today; in front of this computer, fingers tapping madly at my keyboard, talking to you, beautiful someone, and I wouldn't change a thing because if I did, I wouldn't be at this most important place: *here now*.

Today, I look at my body and think, "Okay, we're in this together."

## We literally get only one

Why are we so critical of our bodies? Why do we strive for some arbitrary ideal that shifts anyway? Our bodies are our homes here on Earth. We only get one, and that means we have to take care of it and treat it like we do anything precious, anything that's not just rare, but quite literally one-of-a-kind.

In *Dream Come True*, I pointed out that beauty standards are arbitrary; they change all the time:

> Did you know for example, that early in the 20$^{th}$ century, being zaftig (curvy and voluptuous) was a status symbol? It meant there was an excess of food and leisure time in your life that signaled wealth. Today, despite our efforts to have a more body positive outlook, lean physiques still signal leisure time and/or hard-driving ambition to hit the gym or go for a pre-dawn run.

> Or did you know that at one point, having a tan meant someone was a laborer, a person who had to work in the fields to earn a day's pay and feed their family? Today, a

tan is considered a healthful status symbol, a sign that you have time to play golf or sit in the sun and don't have to work in an office all day.

Not all that long ago, muscles on a woman were considered "unfeminine" (don't *even* get me started).

The point is that from the beginning of time, being different from the currently acceptable standard didn't make you unique or special. It made you weird, and even more often, wrong. Unacceptable. In need of "fixing" to be brought up to par. Literally, to be made *average*.

Still, some things are constant: our bodies get us from here to there. They house our incredible brains, bring us joy like the indescribable pleasure of a loved one's touch or the yum of a silky bite of cheesecake.

They enable us to the feel the refreshing quench of jumping in a pool on a hot day.

Taste the sweetness of a grape. Hear the incredible beauty of a piano solo or an emotional rap classic.

Smell lilacs and the ocean, tangy garlic bread and the sweet hint of Spring in the air after a long Winter.

Some of our bodies have created children, in itself an unimaginable miracle.

Our hands plant and clap and cook and make beds and fold clothes.

# Treat your body like it belongs to someone you love (because it *does*)

The list continues:

Our bodies move us from here to there. Enable us to earn a living. Take care of the people we love. Clean our homes. Some of our bodies have saved the lives of people who were ill, helped people in physical or emotional pain. Our bodies enable our creative ideas to become actual creat*ions* that bring joy and inspiration to the world.

Our vocal chords speak words of love and encouragement, share our convictions and ideas, sing our favorite songs. Our hands play music, type messages that communicate with others, speak in gestures. They paint and draw. Our arms carry babies and cart groceries. They hug and comfort. Our feet dance and drive and skip with joy. Our legs climb stairs and mountains.

I came across these two poems that express these ideas so beautifully, and I encourage you to find and follow these amazing poets. Mariah Hicks concludes her poem "of home" with this beautiful couplet:

> *my body used to sing the blues, but now it*
> *sings of sweet july, now it sings of home.*

In "a place to rest" poet Cheyenne Diaz writes:

> *the war is over;*
> *my body breathes:*
> *welcome home.*

And we only get one. One body. One chance to use it to bring goodness and light to our lives and the lives of our world. When we denigrate it or neglect it, we prevent it from doing these things. I know my body is not who I am (each of us is also soul, intellect, and spirit), but in the meantime, my body does an awful lot of work for me.

As I head at speed to the middle of my life, and as we all together have endured a pandemic, I've become so very conscious of this. This one body, one chance. And how quickly it can be gone. Though we don't like to think about it, there is a time stamp on all this, beautiful someone. It does end.

In the meantime, taking care of our own physiology is an awesome responsibility. Loving it, respecting its amazing power and the work it does every day is essential to our ability to brave our lives, take care of ourselves and the people we love, and contribute our unique gifts to the world.

## Rivers, not lakes

It is, ultimately, one of the greatest forms of authenticity in our lives, to respect the vessels we've been given to live them in. The vessels that have been uniquely designed to enable us to give our one-of-a-kind gifts to the world while we're here. That is their purpose. That is their journey and their ultimate victory. Not to take and get and consume, full stop, but also to give.

It only makes sense, beautiful someone. Why would some of us have such an embarrassment of riches that we can walk on marble floors in an ice cold mall in the middle of August sipping a $5 coffee when other people have to walk in searing heat an hour a day for one pail of water for an entire family? Why do we have enough money to buy a book like this when other people have never been taught to read? Why do I have two computers and a smartphone when children in some families have to go to the library or share a single used laptop to do their homework? Why? Luck of the draw? Accident of birth?

These are the kinds of things that would keep me up at night, wondering, and often feeling guilty and unworthy. After lots of thinking and prayer, I believe that the reason is really simple: it's so that we can do something good with these material gifts, and that doing something good with them is part of our calling, our mission for being here.

In this sense, they are not to be consumed and discarded, but to strengthen and enable us to pass the blessing on, in whatever form that may take: donations of time or resources as well as other forms of generosity: understanding, kindness, the benefit of the doubt. We are not lakes where blessings land and stay. We're rivers through which blessings flow. We need to pass them on.

This is the very essence of a gift. It is surrounded by giving. It was given to us, and it should make us more giving as a result. Think of how you feel when someone gives you a holiday gift and you didn't think to get them something. That's a crummy feeling, right? Here's our chance to always give something back.

## Relaxing into our bodies

When we denigrate our bodies by complaining about their size or shape or age, when we spend time trying so hard to shape and dye and spray and cover, we're implicitly saying our bodies are the wrong size, shape, age, and if we don't perform this masquerade, other people will know (!).

When we pretend we are something we're not (e.g., 30), we are not accepting ourselves, the honest and authentic human we are in the body we've been gifted and the experiences we've both celebrated and endured as the badges of honor we have *earned*. We are telling ourselves, quite literally, "I'm not acceptable as I am" and "My experiences were not worth anything. I learned nothing from them. They have somehow made me weaker, not stronger." That makes our experiences not just worthless but damaging instead of empowering. And beautiful someone, we are performing for a world whose standards of beauty are unreachable or unsustainable, and *constantly changing*.

Let's start there.

Loving our bodies, whether they're tall or short, young or mature. Whether our hair is there or not, richly colored or silver, straight or curly. Whether our skin is smooth and clear or decorated with freckles and earned smile lines and eye twinkles. Whether our joints and muscles are limber or they bark at us after pulling weeds or shoveling snow.

Let's relax into where our bodies are in the parenthesis of time that is our lives. Looking back at all they've done, looking forward to what they will enable us to accomplish in the future. And showing them the kindness and gratitude they deserve.

In *Yes Change Everything!* I included this story:

Getting dressed in the locker room before class, I overhear two women joking about someone who's wearing some seriously bright workout clothes. "I want one of those mirrors," one says with a smirk, "the kind that makes her think that outfit looks good."

I'm aware — the whole gym is aware — of who they're talking about. She's tall, maybe six feet, and super strong. In the weight room, earbuds in, she moves without a word to anyone, picking up huge dumbbells and pumping lots of plates. Afterward, she and her neon tangerine leggings and chartreuse tank top stroll into the studio for a group class. She walks confidently across the floor, head high, shoulders back. Her eyes are clear, her expression open and softly smiling.

Looking at her, I get a little misty-eyed. "I want to be like that. How do you get like that?" I wonder. "Do you just wake up one day after years of professional-grade wall flowering and think, 'Screw it. I'm curvy, I like myself, and I'm going to do, say, and wear what I want'? Or are you born thinking that way? And if you don't have that kind of confidence by the time you're 30, can you get it? Hypnosis maybe? Meds? What is *wrong* with me?"

Because I believe that woman had it right. She liked what she saw in the mirror, and what she knew was under her clothes...herself. Maybe what she was doing was more important than what she was wearing. Maybe she was proud of herself for being able to buy the outfit after saving up for it. Maybe it made her feel a certain way that enabled her to be so confident and self-assured.

Maybe many things.

But you know, big picture, this really didn't have anything to do with whether her outfit worked. It had to do with how she felt, how she carried herself. The high probability that she knew what people were thinking and didn't care. The fact that she probably felt beautiful (focused, powerful, confident) and that for her, that feeling was deeply private and personal. That she only looked in her own mirror and knew her beauty was in the eye of one beholder — herself. No one else's opinion mattered. It was her mirror after all.

## Comfortably self-aware

This story really has nothing to do with this person's reasons for choosing her outfit. It has to do with her deeply private, quiet, and personal view of herself that will *never be fully understood by anyone else*. A feeling that once we have it, helps us be more loving, more giving, and more successful at anything we touch because our insides are right, so our outsides can be too. The isolating agony of self-consciousness becomes confident self-awareness to be part of the world and offer it our uniqueness and beauty.

Maybe most important, this comfortable self-awareness gives us a peace that carries us through every day. We stop wasting time second-guessing ourselves or wondering what others think. We're not wasting energy on losing our way and losing our purpose as we compare ourselves (too often unfavorably) to everyone else.

This positive self-awareness is a kind of soul compass that won't let us lose our way again. Beautiful someone, imagine feeling this kind of peace, this kind of relaxed calm in your body.

"It's taken me years to get to this point, and honestly not only has it been a bumpy road, I'm still a work in progress in this department," said Laura who has vitiligo. "Owning the uniqueness of my skin and seeing it as something positive, not a deficit, not less than other people, not outside the mainstream and therefore illegitimate in some way — because in addition to my vitiligo, I've made some unconventional choices around jobs, fitness, hobbies, friendships, and more — is a life-long practice for me. Although definitely, on my best days I go after my passions, spend time in my studio, 'sing like I don't need the money and dance like no one's watching.' I am doing my best to own my uniqueness, vitiligo and all. It's just that fighting a lifetime of being scary weird, not being good enough and not deserving isn't an easy thing to do."

I thank my friend Laura from the bottom of my heart for sharing something so personal. I know it wasn't easy because she's a very private person. She's also extraordinarily loving, creative, interesting, decent and unique. And I don't think I'm being dramatic when I say that depriving me and everyone else of all her beauty just to fit into a world that won't understand it really scares me.

A long time ago, someone told me that one of the surest ways to make ourselves crazy is to compare our insides (our real private selves with which we are intimately familiar) with everyone else's outsides: with their show, their edited-for-primetime stories and pictures. We know our own insides but we only see others' outsides, which are often carefully manufactured for visibility to the world around them. It's such an unfair comparison, and I thank the person who told me this because it is such a liberating reality.

One of our mantras, beautiful someone, is that we don't do crazy anymore! And so let's work on this together, owning our uniqueness seeing it as something precious and special placed in us for a reason. Most of all, let's never put it down as unattractive or not good enough just to be popular with people who honestly are probably doing the exact same thing.

DIANA DAVIN

## Let only love in

Dismiss whatever insults your soul.

— Walt Whitman

For his film *Super-Size Me*, Morgan Spurlock, a 33-year-old documentary filmmaker who started his project in good health, wanted to see the effects of junk food on our bodies. For a month, Spurlock decided he would eat nothing but burgers, shakes, and <u>lots</u> of fries. To give the film credibility and get a scientific read on the effects of eating this food for 30 days, Spurlock hired three doctors to monitor his health throughout the project.

In the end, his physicians documented effects that could only be called shocking — even to them — including dangerously elevated cholesterol, nausea, stomach and chest pains, liver damage, and eventually (no surprise) depression. Spurlock took the time to document something we know intuitively: junk food is bad for us, but now we know: it's *really* bad.

Sweets and treats like shakes and fries are fine once in a while. But our bodies can't take a constant barrage of nutritionless food. Which is why none of us should try the *Super-Size Me* "diet," however tempting fast food is!

But we "consume" other things too: media, conversations, and definitely the energy from relationships. All this comes toward our beautiful lives, sometimes minute-by-minute. So we face daily, even hourly choices about what we let into our heads, and into our lives.

A steady diet of negative headlines, sensational but ultimately uninspiring news stories ("If it bleeds, it leads," is the saying in journalism, meaning the more fantastically negative a story is, the higher above the fold/screen break it will be) and sad endings are seriously unhealthy.

## M&Ms and Reese's Pieces

Maybe we think, "Nah, I can handle it." But think about this: it's an old enough story to have made it into the annals of film folklore, but when the movie *ET* was in development, producer Steven Spielberg approached the Mars Corporation with the idea of making M&Ms the alien ET's candy of choice in the movie.

Mars declined, so Spielberg approached Hershey's with the same idea. They accepted, and Reese's Pieces became ET's favorite candy. The technique is called product placement: the use of packaged products in visual media as a way to increase sales of these products, and it's a really effective part of a brand's sales and marketing strategy.

How effective?

When *ET* hit theaters, sales of Reese's Pieces, which had been floundering until that point, jumped 80 percent and stayed there. Moviegoers were influenced not just to associate positive emotions with the candy, but to go out and buy it — lots of it.

Just as we take in physical nutrition through eating, we "feed" our minds what we consume through our eyes and ears. Every minute of every day, we choose what we will permit into our lives because every Netflix binge, every podcast, book, and article feeds us information, ideas, preconceptions, and images which eventually morph into points of view and desires.

Too much negative information is at the very least, distracting. Too much can also be unbearable. If I focus too much on pain and suffering in the headlines, I can't function, and I definitely can't write about hope and health for us. Seriously, beautiful someone, if a lot of what we see and hear every day is relentlessly negative, who could possibly have the emotional stamina — or any tangible reason for that matter — to feel strong, confident and hopeful?

Unfortunately, negative information, the kind that scares us, touches a part of our brains that pays attention: alarms go off. We move to protect ourselves and the people we love with lopsided, impulsive decisions based on fear. When our brains are functioning this way, they don't take the time to balance the scary information with positive possibilities, which are always there if we have the emotional stamina to look for them.

This is an area I've had to do a lot of work on because for some reason, it's really hard for me to watch something without being affected by it. I saw the movie *Saving Private Ryan* when it came out and couldn't get over the unbearably soul-stirring story for months. (I'm probably still not over it.) Don't believe this doesn't happen to you! Maybe not to the same degree, but it most definitely does; it must, whether on a conscious level or not.

For all these reasons, we should be incredibly careful about what enters our bodies through our precious senses. And good news: we have almost complete control over this. That doesn't mean we're immune to negativity. The bad boss may still come our way. The difficult customer might still skewer us by surprise for one reason or another. We may still be given the "gift" of someone's unconstructive criticism or be accused of something we didn't do.

It's just that we can decide, *before* we let someone's negativity into our souls or read a story that makes us feel hopeless, whether we want to let this information in or not. Beautiful someone, we need to have the ultimate courage to stand guard at the doors of our minds. No one else can do this for us. And it's actually an easy job: if it's encouraging, inspiring, balanced, and ultimately hope-filled, it's in. Otherwise, not so much.

## Sturdy hope

A favorite quote by poet Walt Whitman is posted in front of me. It is not an exaggeration to say that these lines from his poem *Song of the Open Road* were a vital spark for Blossie's Books:

> *Afoot and light-hearted I take to the open road,*
> *Healthy, free, the world before me,*
> *The long brown path before me leading wherever I choose.*

The beauty of this statement that so affects me is layered: of course I love the idea of heading wherever we choose, the sense of freedom and possibility. But I also love the image of running barefoot down a long brown path, heart light and eyes shining with excitement about the future and its possibilities.

The latter part of Whitman's life was characterized by a sense of freedom from the constraints of society's expectations. If you read his work, it's easy to draw a clear line between his earlier and later poems, written after he found his true self, and passionately and productively embraced it. And so when I read that he once said, borne of his own life experience, that we should "Dismiss whatever insults our souls," it hits with a jolt.

For *Braving It*, our take on Whitman's wise counsel is to *let only love in*. And from the jump, let's be super-clear: this is not about expecting to be treated like royalty or ensuring that nothing harsh ever crosses our paths, or being incensed when it does. Of course that's ridiculous. The world is complex, and there is as much negative energy and outright evil as we can handle, and then some.

We can't ignore it, because if we try to pretend that it doesn't exist, things will not go well. It will enter our lives anyway, as aggression, exploitation, dishonesty, or cruelty, and find us smiling sweetly and unprepared. At times we have to deal with it — head on — and process it after the fact to figure out what we learned and what we can do next.

When someone is angry or upset, we don't have to run away like some fragile princess who can't handle controversy. In fact, sometimes turning to face a confrontation is the most loving thing we can do.

The hope that we talk about together in Blossie's Books is up to the task. Far from fragile, our hope is sturdy and strong. This hope knows that we need to be positive in spite of setbacks and in the face of obstacles. It would deeply trouble me, beautiful someone (my heart to yours) if any of what we work on together seemed to be suggesting that we faint at any sign of trouble or live in denial of what's real.

No one is entitled to a life free from negativity. When it rains, it rains over everyone's house. We all have to pay taxes. Facing tough circumstances, dealing with soul-sucking situations, impossible people at work, thoughtlessness even in our own families — all this and more is just part of being alive.

At the same time, it's not okay to ignore it all. Injustice, dishonesty, cruelty…they're all very real, and sticking our heads in the sand like an ostrich is not a life strategy.

So, letting only love in doesn't mean ignoring anyone or anything negative, especially when our souls are telling us this wouldn't be right.

Handling adversity is an important way in which we learn to live honestly and bravely. And, beautiful someone, our hope is strong enough and then some to do it.

## Soul space

Letting only love in refers to what we allow to take up space in our souls. What we are metabolizing spiritually. Negative circumstances need to be handled with love and respect, sometimes with strength, sometimes even confrontationally, but letting only love in means we don't allow them to take up residence inside us. And when we're done with them, we're *done* with them. We won't allow them to use our hearts as their permanent address.

Let's stand bravely at the door of our lives and choose what we allow in. So we don't have to do the hard, exhausting work of evicting the daily onslaught of fear and anger and despair that comes at us. Instead, we never let them in in the first place. We acknowledge that they're there, deal with them as we must, and move on.

We don't allow anyone or anything to enter the sacred space that is our soul, our inner life — the part of us that houses our ideas, our dreams, our hopes — unless they come in love: with good intention, helpful ideas, and positive energy. Then, we go out into the world with loving confidence to live boldly. No need to waste energy evicting anything because we didn't let it in in the first place.

Let's take it deeper dive into what *let only love in* means.

To illustrate this concept, I present: Josh.

## Josh's invisi-fence

*Yes Changes Everything* includes these paragraphs under the heading, "Space in our lives is a privilege":

> When we think about what saying yes can do in our lives, everything that it can introduce and enable and create and inspire, it's easy to see that the ability to choose yes really is a superpower that needs to be treated like one. We can't just throw the door open, say yes, and let anything saunter into our lives unexamined and unchecked.
>
> Instead, we need to respect that when we choose to say yes, we are literally opening the door wide to let experiences and people and opportunities into our lives — that's a sacred space that they are entering! Being part of our lives is a privilege. That's not to sound arrogant; it's just to

acknowledge that in order to stay healthy and happy and free to care for and contribute to our families, friends, jobs, communities (not to mention ourselves!), we need to view our lives as precious.

"When I read that in *Yes Changes Everything*," Josh said, "I was like, yesss!" Josh has what he calls his invisible fence, a truly liberating concept that goes something like this: "Come to me with love and respect, and you're in. Approach me with anything else, and I'll make it seem as if I'm listening intently, but I won't be. I'll make it seem as if I will take your negative ideas to heart, but I won't. And I'll make it seem as if I'll allow you into my life, but honestly I won't. Because I will only let people into my life who respect and support me, not necessarily agree with me, but whose disagreement comes from love and with respect, and nothing less."

Space in our lives *is* precious, and we need to treat it that way. "It's taken me a long time to realize that a lot of the pain I've experienced arrived in my life from the outside," said Josh. "They weren't things I did, nothing that I said, and definitely nothing I deserved. They were *external* to me. They came from other people, unlucky situations I got swept into, a sense of misplaced responsibility that was dropped on me by people who were benefiting from my selflessness. Until I read your book, I didn't have the emotional awareness to understand this and not feel guilty. Now I see that these situations that made me feel so bad were <u>not my fault</u>. They were outside of me, and that meant they could actually stay there! I could keep them there. I didn't *have* to let them in. They weren't mine. They belonged to someone or something else. That's how I finally decided to be much more careful about what — and who — I let in."

Like Josh, our own brave souls need invisible fences. If we want to live courageously, we can't open the door to just anything or anyone who wants to take up space in our hearts. Anything/anyone who's not loving and respectful has no place in our brave lives. They may show up and need to be handled, but they can't get in. We say no, and we certainly kick to the curb anything that's managed to get in that's not healthy, constructive, hope filled, and guilt-free.

## Love is the opposite of fear

Beautiful someone, we often think that courage is the opposite of fear. But in Blossie's dictionary, the opposite of fear is love. Think of the feelings that circle around fear. What are we afraid of? Pain, hurt, loss, insolvency — things that make us scared, sad, maybe resentful. So we "prepare" to face these fears by making ourselves indifferent, guarded, or sometimes even aggressive. "That'll do it," we think. "I'm ready now. Nothing's going to catch me off guard again." We're ready for whatever adversary might be around the corner.

But this is not courage. This is indifference. This is aggression. And it's totally understandable when hurt or loss have found us in the past. The phrase, "Never again," has become our mantra. It's just that indifference and aggression aren't really going to help. They can't keep us from making impulsive decisions or fighting back when we don't really have to. Or making snap judgments about someone — and being wrong.

And indifference and aggression can't prevent the regret we feel afterward.

Only love can do that.

So, "Never again" definitely. It's just the *how* that matters.

## Love grows

Only love can help us move away from fear. A firm, concerted, conscious decision to allow into our brains and our bodies things that are life-affirming, kind, interesting, respectful, fascinating, positive, healthy.

So what should make it through our souls' screening process if our invisible fence is only supposed to let love in? I think that's simple but not always easy.

Here's how we recognize love, beautiful someone:

*Love grows (increases, expands, adds, challenges) while fear contracts (decreases, contracts, diminishes) us.*

That means love builds up. It closes wounds. It radiates. It empowers. It inspires. It is constructive. It builds.

It's goodness that expands.

It's kindness that heals.

It's warmth that radiates.

It's trust that empowers.

It's fresh ideas that inspire.

It's respect for differences that stimulate and educate.

It's feedback that's truly constructive and helps us build a better next time.

It's hard work that creates something good and positive and helpful.

It's devotion that supports and makes others feel safe.

Love makes things better. It makes *us* better. It includes tough love sometimes but tough love that aims to make a person or situation ultimately better. Love expands — it is full of ideas and helpful advice. It's generous and expects nothing in return. It starts a chain reaction in us that makes us want to be generous with other people, rather than sucking all the energy and the life out of us so that we have nothing left for anyone else.

Love changes us for the better, and then we change things for the better.

Love of our work expands our horizons, sharpens our thinking, makes us believe in what's possible, what we can create.

Love of other people respects their differences, gives them the benefit of the doubt, and connects us to them in an ever-expanding circle of positive relationships.

Love of our communities deepens our sense of responsibility and expands our involvement in making our neighborhoods better places to live.

## Only love may enter here

Starting right here and now: we will live boldly and bravely by putting up a sign over the door to our souls that says, "Only love may enter here." And so, we will not let people or experiences into our lives that are not uplifting. Nothing will enter that's cruel or makes us doubt ourselves and our strengths. If people or experiences aren't healthy and loving, they pass through our lives — we will handle them as we must — but then they'll leave. They won't live in our souls and waste our precious energy.

So, let's...

> Limit our commitments to those that really matter and are necessary.
>
> Be exquisitely careful about who we give access to our soul.
>
> Exercise our "no" muscle so it doesn't get flabby. "No, I can't be there." "I'm sorry, I won't be able to help." "No, I'm not going to do that."
>
> Fill our minds with positive ideas and energy on a regular basis by reading, watching, and following accounts that uplift and transport us to healthy, hopeful places.
>
> This is the energy, the velocity of love that we need to let into our lives, the kind that touches us and immediately starts to grow, to germinate and radiate good energy.

## And definitely...let's turn off unhelpful voices

There are so many voices to listen to. There are voices we need to hear:

The voices of people in need.

The subsonic voice of our kids' hurts and fears that we hear more clearly than anybody.

Voices we want to hear:

The voice of love from our partner.

The voice of genuine compliments or recognition.

The voice of opportunity we don't want to miss.

Then there are the destructive voices:

The voice of the past pain and mistakes.

The business voice about what a "true professional" should do, usually something we are not already doing.

The soul-sucking voices in our heads whose only purpose is to remind us of the negative things that can and did happen to us last time we tried something similar.

The voices that tell us not to trust ourselves, but instead to listen to them as the truth.

The voices that tell us what to do in service of them.

We hear them all, and when we're at our best, we discern the loving voices from the destructive ones and then put own heart and soul into our decision making. *When we're at our best.* When we're not, we give the negative voices too much power.

Let's start to develop a unique sensitivity to the voices we need to hear and want to hear. We can let these in; we can let them spark good action in ourselves. At the same time, we can hear the destructive voices without taking them to heart — because we let only love in.

Beautiful someone, letting only love in his some of the greatest and most challenging soul work we can do. It's also quite possibly the most important as we brave our lives.

## Stop explaining!

> Silence is a source of great strength.
>
> — Lao Tzu

A while ago, I went to a Confident Communication workshop that included this unforgettable exercise:

We sat expectantly in our seats as the moderator asked for a volunteer from the audience, let's call her Michele. They stood on the stage together as the moderator asked Michele whether she would be willing to give (not *lend*) him $1,000. "No, not really," she answered, a little sheepishly.

The moderator asked, "Why not?"

Michele began, "Because I don't really know you and —"

"No!" The moderator yelled at her with a smile.

Michele jumped back, smiled, then giggled uncomfortably, but she did stop talking.

Then the moderator asked whether Michele would like to face the audience and share the most embarrassing memory of her life with them.

Michele giggled again, and said, "No, I wouldn't."

Again, the moderator asked, "Why not?"

Michele responded, "Because that would make me really uncomfortable and I —"

"No!" The moderator yelled at her again and smiled.

This pattern went on a few more times as the moderator asked Michele whether she'd be willing to do one difficult, impossible, or embarrassing thing after another (including eating a bowl of live crickets). And every time Michele responded to his question about why or why not by beginning to explain herself, he would shout "No!" with a smile.

Eventually even the audience realized that the goal was for Michele not to explain herself, but instead say no and nothing more. Michele finally caught on, and the audience roared our approval.

It was one of the most memorable experiences of my life.

Beautiful someone, we don't need to explain ourselves anywhere near as often as we think we do, and that's difficult especially when someone is in our face demanding an explanation for a choice that we're making.

As a general suggestion, the times when we are required to offer an explanation are limited to our closest circle of intimate relationships (and I mean our closest, smallest circle), and maybe our manager at work (maybe...sometimes we don't need to provide an explanation for why we're not coming in, why we're late, why we would like to take vacation at a certain time;

these are judgment calls and the subject of a different Blossie@work! book ☺).

Not explaining ourselves is definitely an exercise in self-respect, but it's also a key part of taking responsibility for ourselves and our choices, and *that* beautiful someone, is the courageous connection.

## Asking for approval

Almost always, we feel the urge to explain ourselves in situations where we need to refuse a request or decline an offer. It's as if we can't honor our own choices *unless* we 1.) have a legit reason, and 2.) the person we are explaining ourselves to accepts that reason as legit. In this way, explaining ourselves is absolutely asking for approval. If they say it's okay, it is. If they don't, it's not, and we need to come up with a better reason that they approve of or, worse, capitulate to keep the peace.

We're in effect, delegitimizing our choices by requiring another person's approval for them. In a one-on-one relationship, this also sets up a dynamic that we owe the other person an explanation for everything we do, and maybe worse: that we need their approval to run our own lives.

Approval-seeking also sends a message to *us* that we have to explain our boundaries to others' satisfaction, or we have no right to them. That we owe the world an explanation of our identity and dreams. And here's the rub: unless the world grants us its approval, we have no right to claim our dreams. If we give this right to the world, the world will take it.

Over time, we begin to feel victimized. If we're only moving ahead with what we want based on other people's opinions, it's only natural that we start to feel subjugated. Beautiful someone, whenever we feel like a victim, it's a sure bet that we've given our power away. We're not braving our lives, living them courageously according to our own priorities and values, with the confidence that this alignment is, in itself, all the approval we need.

When we seek approval, we're letting someone else determine what we do. But when we *stop* explaining ourselves (i.e., stop freely handing out information about ourselves and/or our motives that people don't need or shouldn't have), we start to live courageously because we're no longer indirectly asking for permission for what we do or choose not to do.

## Confident, not confrontational

Whether it's a nip-in-the-bud situation or one that's progressed all the way to enough-is-enough, our freedom to make choices without explaining ourselves is essential to braving our lives. Still, our delivery of this all-important messaging matters.

We want to sound confident, not confrontational.

A few suggestions:

*Don't hedge.* Hedging takes different forms. Sometimes we may ask for permission to refuse, for example: "Would you mind terribly if I said no?" or "Would it be okay if I sat this one out?"

Minimizing a statement before we make it is another example:

- "You may not agree, but…"

- "This isn't going to make you happy, but…"
- "This is going to sound weird, but…"
- "You're probably not going to appreciate this, but…"

Hedges are for gardens, not our brave lives! Let's listen for these evasive habits in our refusals and stop them before we say them.

*Be aware of body language.* We know from countless studies that a whopping 93 percent of our message is communicated through tone of voice and body language, and only 7 percent through the words we use. So when we're saying no without explaining ourselves, our voice and mannerisms should be confident, but not antagonistic.

Stand tall, shoulders down and back. Relax your arms and hands (no crossed arms or clenched fists). Don't fidget with pens, paperclips, or change in your pocket. Look directly at the person as you talk, raise your eyebrows slightly, smile and nod if appropriate.

Remember that your voice has a body language all its own. Keep it clear and calm. Breathe deeply to give your voice energy and strength. Don't rush to get the words out. This practice also helps us look relaxed and thoughtful, not scared and uncomfortable.

Be sure to put a period – not a question mark – at the end of your refusal. Rather than, "I have another appointment at that time?" or "My fee for this work would be $5,000?" make these statements declarative: "I have another appointment at that time." "My fee for this work would be $5,000." This leaves room for conversation, just not for debate.

There will be times when a direct and simple, "Stop that" is necessary. If your integrity is under attack, for example, or if someone is treating you in an unethical way, you need to put a stop to it with a crystal clear:

- "That makes me uncomfortable. Please don't do it again."
- "I take exception to that comment. Please don't say that to me again."

In these situations, clarity is key. Look directly at the person, lower your pitch, and say it like you mean it.

## Finesse...plus

Some refusals require even more finesse:

You sincerely wish you could help in a tough situation, and though you can't, you're still willing to help in the future.

You've decided that going to the event doesn't work this time, but you want to be invited next time.

You can't help out with this project, but you want to stay on the short list for the next one.

While you need to refuse, you've got to do it in a way that extends an hand for the future:

- "I can't help right now, but thanks for confiding in me, and please keep me posted. I might be able to help out in the future."
- "No, but I'd really like a rain check."

- "I can't help out right now, but I'd like to in the future. Can I stay in touch?"

After your refusal, keep the tone light and reassure the person that you're refusing the offer, not rejecting them. Some phrases to keep at the ready:

- "It was really nice of you to ask."
- "Thanks for thinking of me."
- "Great to know you wanted me to be there!"

## And finally, remember less is more

Whether it's to decline an invitation, to disagree, or to change a date, we don't owe people an explanation anywhere near as often we might think. To break the habit of explaining ourselves, one simple rule works wonders: *less is more*. TMI (too much information) hands someone the tools to ask for more information or an explanation.

Here's how this works.

Compare a "naked no," a refusal without an explanation (a simple "No thank you" for example) with the TMI version of the same statement: "I won't be able to make it because I have to get ready for a large shipment at work that's coming in late on Thursday."

In the first case, no means no. Not much to talk about because the naked no doesn't leave the door open for discussion or give someone room to ask for more information.

In the TMI version, we've practically invited the person to say, "Thursday? That's three days away! You can take a quick break before then to help me" or "What do you need to do to get ready, and how much time will it take? I'm sure you can find a few minutes to spare. Get back to me and let me know what time this afternoon is good."

TMI implies that we're insecure about our position.

Note the differences:

| Less is more... | TMI... |
|---|---|
| *"I can't be there. I've got something else scheduled."* | "I'm not sure, but I think I have a meeting with the Sales team that I've had on my schedule for like a month." |
| *"I won't be able to help with that."* | "Any other day, I would! I just can't today because I need to leave for an appointment at 4." |
| *"I'd rather not, thanks."* | "I've never liked those types of events. I went once and had a horrible time. So I'd just rather not this time." |
| *"I need to get back to work right now."* | "If I don't get back to work in the next 10 minutes, I'll never finish my report on time. I've already gotten one extension on the deadline because of that problem I had when I got back from San Francisco." |

Notice how confident and clear the "less is more" responses sound compared to the TMI responses. There's just zero wiggle room in a simple, "No thanks." As a bonus, we sound so much more confident in the "less is more" space. We're showing people that we respect our time and priorities. They will respond by respecting them too.

Practice saying "no" without explaining yourself on something small, like why you want to return something to a store. If the salesperson asks why, just answer in a breezy tone, "Oh it just wasn't right." If you need to change a dentist appointment and are asked why, don't give information about your schedule like, "Well, I had to take off two days last week when my pool was being installed, and if I take one more personal day, I'm in trouble!" Keep it simple: "This time no longer works."

After these small, zero-risk refusals, expand to more challenging issues like staying late every day at work or doing a favor for someone that would just put too much on your plate.

DIANA DAVIN

## Shhh...listen!

Intuition is the whisper of the soul.

— Jiddu Krishnamurti

Beautiful someone, you may remember these paragraphs from *Yes Changes Everything!*:

Sometimes, a choice may seem right, all the intellectual facts support going ahead with it...

- He/she says all the right things.
- The job in Chicago has great benefits, good opportunities for advancement, and the company will pay for relocation.
- The apartment we want to buy is close to work, spacious, and available for the right price.

Still, for some reason, we hesitate.

There's the temptation to say, "What is *wrong* with me — this is so perfect! I think I'm just being a wimp about it." But beautiful someone, when we hesitate, there's a reason. Something is going on intuitively that we need to trust and pay attention to.

You know how we tell our kids that if they ever feel uncomfortable in a situation — afraid, queasy, weirded out in any way — they *must* trust that feeling and walk away, or say no, or call us, or all three? Lately with my own kids I've started to shorthand it: "Listen to your gut — it never lies." And it's true that our brains sometimes rationalize, "reason" things out, or make excuses, but our stomachs can't do these things. Which is why when our guts are talking to us, they are telling the truth.

**Genius**
Our intuition is a form of genius and listening to it means that we respect the limits of the supercomputer in our heads. As the master craftsperson of our own lives, sometimes we need to put the tool (brain) back in the toolbox and just trust our guts.

The need to listen to our own internal promptings is more important today that ever, with the mind-blowing number of external stimuli coming at us every hour of every day. Looking across a variety of estimates, in 2021 the average person was exposed to 6,000 to 10,000 ads every day. And that's just *ads*...doesn't count videos, texts, games, apps, emails, and everything else. All coming from outside of us. All with the intention of motivating actions, some of which are in our good interests, and some diametrically opposed to them.

So we don't go crazy running after every ideal (often edited and so, fake), product or service (ads can make literally *anything* sound great) that all this external stimulation puts in front of us, we've got to take deliberate charge of our brains, our hearts, and our choices. Which brings me to the point of this chapter...

## Inside out

Beautiful someone, this is so important: living bravely is an inside-out proposition.

This means we pay attention and honor our inner promptings…

- We listen to ideas and suggestions from people we trust, but ultimately we make our own decisions based on what's right for us and the people we care about.
- We live by our own values and conscience, regardless of what we're being tempted to do from the outside, whether that's by people or ads or anything else.
- We trust our instincts when we feel that an idea, person, or course of action isn't right for us.
- We believe our hearts when they've been broken, not allowing anyone to convince us that abuse or a painful experience "wasn't that bad" or "was such a long time ago" and we should "just get over it."
- We're peaceful no matter what's going on outside us.
- We accept that bad things happen, and while we can fight to make a difference for causes we believe in, we understand our own limits, and don't try to (and fail and be frustrated when we can't) fix everything within a five-mile radius of us.
- We can be okay even when the people around us are not.

This is just a partial list, but when we do these things and others like them, when we trust our instincts, not only do we live bravely, we are happier, healthier, and saner for it.

## "It took me a lifetime"

Codependence is such a pervasive problem that there's a good chance you've heard this word as well as related terms such as enabling behavior, relationship imbalance, personality disorder, and more.

I'm not an expert who has studied these principles academically, and so I would suggest reading some of the many amazing resources on these terms and this spectrum of choices if you feel that that would be valuable to you. There are also thousands of helpful videos covering these important topics as well as those related to them such as narcissism, borderline personality disorder, covert behavior, and the like.

I have however learned a lot about this topic from many years of personal experience. And so in this section in particular, I am writing from my heart to yours.

In everyday terms, a codependent relationship is one that's out of balance. One person is *needed* and the other is *needy*. When we're the needed (a role you and I are more likely to play in a relationship), we work hard to please people at our own expense by making a set of externally-driven choices in our lives that most definitely stand in the way of our own authenticity and honest dreams as surely as any solid brick wall.

Worst case, codependence makes us a chameleon — not our true selves, not listening to our inner voice or honoring our natural and authentic instincts, but rather someone who changes to fit the needs of the moment and keep others happy. We become unwilling to trust ourselves and worry that our choices, whatever they are, aren't right.

Codependence is thinking that our values, needs, and plans are not as important as everyone else's, that keeping other people happy matters more than anything, often regardless of how unreasonable or unfair or impromptu their demands are.

Codependence comes from fear of disappointing someone. Of having to deal with someone's anger. Of being discarded by them when we make choices based on our inner promptings and thus don't do what they want.

And for all these reasons, codependence does not represent our true selves and can't be part of our brave and authentic lives.

"It took me a lifetime," Stella said, "to understand that living for other people, more to the point living as if the happiness of everyone who comes into my life, even briefly, is all that really matters, is definitely not living bravely. It isn't even living honestly. Because while there are definitely people in our lives who care enough about us to make *our* needs a priority, there are many more people who don't do this. So feeling responsible and taking care of everyone who crosses my path doesn't make sense as a long-term livable lifestyle."

Stella was finally able to understand why she was so stressed all the time when one day she took a notebook and a pencil and sat in a park. "Once I had that stillness and quiet time," she said, "I realized that every single stressful situation I was writing about was literally someone else's. I was worried about my friend, my fiancé, my mom, and what they were going through, and here's the kicker: feeling guilty if I didn't have a solution to their problems. It wasn't a long leap to realize that I felt like if I couldn't fix it all, I was a failure."

But Stella's misplaced sense of responsibility didn't end with her close relationships. It ranged far and wide. "I realized I was stressed about fixing other people's situations," she said, "including my landlord. The guy I saw at CVS who couldn't find something he needed. Someone who got cut off on the highway that it was suddenly my responsibility to drive next to and let in front of me on purpose. My friend's cousin who was having a biopsy in a couple weeks. My sister-in-law's job headaches. Basically, if it was happening within a 50-mile radius of me, I felt responsible."

What Stella finally understood in those quiet hours at the park was that living this way, "codependent with the world" as she put it, was not only totally crazy-making — we can't possibly fix everything around us, and so we just go crazy trying — it also wasn't even fair to the people around her. The more we try to do for other people, the less they do for themselves, and whether they are conscious of it or not, they're becoming dependent on our selflessness.

When we put ourselves in the middle of situations that really have nothing to do with us, we're *not* actually helping because often we won't have the tools or the knowledge or the time and energy to help in a way that makes a positive difference and so may end up making things worse. Basically, we're involving ourselves in situations that are quite literally none of our business. So the person we're trying to help doesn't win, we certainly don't win, and then we have to ask ourselves — what exactly was the point of all that?

We end up stressed, exhausted, and ineffective to boot. A selfless doormat.

## "You're there, and I'm here"

Of course there's more to codependence than what we willingly take on. Sometimes there are people in our lives who, by virtue of their lack of self-awareness (in the best case) or deliberate manipulation (in the worst case), encourage our unhealthy selflessness and codependence. They drop their problems at our feet expecting us to rise to the occasion and take them on. But beautiful someone, all this does is take energy away from the things we *should* be doing and *want* to be doing and are *responsible* for doing for the people in our lives who truly do need us.

A long time ago I learned a phrase that I use to this day when I feel myself slipping into a codependent situation: "You're there, and I'm here." This is accompanied by a hand gesture that literally pushes away the energy coming at me that's demanding I receive it and get to work on fixing it.

"We are separate," I tell myself. "I don't have to receive your problems into my being and fix them for you any more than you have to receive mine and fix them for me." This doesn't mean that I don't care about the person or even love them in some cases. It just means that I am making the choice not to be responsible for fixing their problems.

It also doesn't mean that I won't help if I can in ways that are genuinely constructive. It means I am protecting myself from overwhelm and helping them take healthy responsibility for their own stuff. So they can solve it and learn and watch themselves grow as they rise to meet their own genuine challenges. In some ways, it is the most loving thing I can do.

You may have heard the term *being an enabler*. This is what it means: by taking on someone else's problems, we are enabling them to have their problems. By taking the responsibility off their shoulders and working on it for them, we are making it possible and eventually acceptable, for them *not to do anything*. We are literally enabling the problem and disabling the person experiencing it.

Chances are they will step into the same choppy waters again and again if they are not made to take responsibility for doing so. There's also a good chance we won't fix their problem well or completely and may even make things worse.

It's interesting that a lot of times when I feel overwhelmed and stalled in my life, honest-to-goodness, just like Stella, there's some measure of codependence going on that's contributing to those feelings. I am being forced (forcing myself?) out of guilt to do something for someone that I know is not going to be helpful, that is going to cost me weeks of energy and that will not be appreciated or healthy for either one of us.

## The guilt trip

And that's important to explore: one of the ways that we can be certain that our actions are in a codependent loop with someone is that the person is not grateful for our help, but instead has come to see it as a kind of entitlement, something that we *have* to do or *owe* them out of some oddly-placed sense of responsibility to them. They're family, they did that thing for us five years ago, they can't help themselves (rarely true), they've been so nice to us...

Be very careful, beautiful someone, about being in relationships where the vibe or even the spoken word is some sense of obligation or quid pro quo (literally, an even exchange: *this* for *that*). I say to the people in my life who I love, "You owe me nothing. You are not obligated to me. You don't have to do anything for me or 'pay me back.'" Love is not a currency. It should never be subject to an "even exchange."

This is the essence of the guilt trip, isn't it? A sense of obligation, of owing someone whether that's actions, money, loyalty, or explanations. And if we don't supply these things to their satisfaction (which is almost always a moving target and rarely clearly defined), then we are selfish, greedy people who aren't grateful for whatever it is we've been given. This is the difference between a gift and a debt. The gift is given with no expectation of anything in return. That's what makes it a *gift*. Guilt trips are about debts, about things that are demanded of us that we "owe" someone else based on their perception of "who they are" or "all they have done for us."

And so, beautiful someone, I offer us this: *we are okay*. We are enough. We are worth more than what we can do for other people. We don't need to feel guilty every time someone around us is struggling. We are not responsible for fixing the world's problems, and we are not guilty when we don't.

When we live boldly, we acknowledge these truths and honor our independence (as opposed to codependence). We also honor our choice to be helpful in a constructive way to people who can really benefit from our help. We do not go on guilt trips and we cannot be manipulated out of walking the path of our bold, brave lives at someone else's bidding.

It's healthy for us and everyone we care about to distance ourselves from situations and people who are making unreasonable demands on our time, our values, our precious energy, and our inner voice.

DIANA DAVIN

## Face it

> You never know how strong
> you are until being strong
> is your only choice.
>
> — Bob Marley

When a family friend lost his job, I puzzled over why he struggled to stay busy every minute with tasks and details of everyday life. He had just lost the only job he'd ever had. He was pushing 50 and had worked at his company — more like a family to him — for 25 years. He literally grew up there. Met his wife there. Built a department from scratch and with a lot of passion.

A new boss had taken an immediate dislike to him and very quickly engineered his firing.

This was huge! Didn't he want to stop and think about his life and what had happened? What was next for him, what he'd learned? My approach would have been to get angry, cry and mourn the loss, and then write about what happened, think it through, probably talk to people I love and trust about it, pouring my heart out until I understood it and figured out my next steps. I'd need to be sure I closed that chapter with a deep understanding of what happened so I could move on as a whole and healthy person — knowledgeable, awake, and aware. This would be essential for me to make sure that this experience became a step of growth and progress in my life.

I finally realized though that for my friend, the point of staying busy *was to stay busy*, exactly because he didn't *want* to think. The whole experience was just too painful for him. He didn't want to reflect and consider and figure out what it all meant. He didn't want to face the pain of being rejected and dismissed by a company and all the people in it who had meant so much to him. He lost a huge part of his identity when he was fired. And it wasn't in some mass layoff either. He had been singled out and let go in a very personal way.

Don't we all do this to some extent though? When tough stuff comes up, rather than deal with it, we get busy with something else or go online to make an appointment, or maybe jump down a YouTube rabbit hole for an hour.

More positively, we may busy ourselves with other stuff when we should be reaching for a goal that seems too big or too long-term or otherwise overwhelming.

Beautiful someone, I do it, more often than I'd like to admit. But I know that when I don't face whatever problem or issue a positive, proactive way, when I run away from something in fear or out of just not wanting to deal, I am at my most vulnerable to it. I'm not living courageously in the face of whatever it is. *It* is in control, not *me* and *my* heart and *my* goals.

The Māori, the indigenous people of New Zealand, have a proverb: "Face the sun and the shadows fall behind you." Let's start using this as a mantra in our lives. That we will not, like my friend who lost his job, hide from what we are challenged with in our lives. We will face it and take whatever action we need to dispense with this thing that is blocking our way forward and hindering our ability to live bravely.

## On silence and sunlight

Friends and I got out of the car at a remote trailhead, and you know that phrase "the silence was deafening"? It really was. The complete lack of sound was so profound that it literally felt like pressure on our eardrums.

We started the hike, and I wondered about all the things that happen in silence. A baby's heart starts beating. Seeds germinate and plants grow. When our minds are silent, solutions to even the toughest problems come to light. Memories long hidden shoot to the surface. In silence, we pray and meditate and understand. Silence is one of the most powerful forces on earth.

And we don't create silence. We *allow* it by turning absolutely everything off. And then it's there for us, a deep and abiding blessing available at any time.

Since it's impossible to solve a problem we don't understand, allowing ourselves the silence to explore it, find its root causes, and make changes that aren't aimed just at symptoms, but rather actual problems...

*Symptom:* Arguing with our significant other about weekend plans
*Actual problem:* Not enough time with our own friends

*Symptom:* Running out of money before the end to the month
*Actual problem:* Unconscious spending on little things we really don't need but give us comfort when we're sad or stressed

*Symptom*: Never getting to the gym or working out
*Actual problem*: We're stuck in a workout rut

...this unique kind of clarity happens so much more readily in silence – a.k.a. *time to think*.

Clarity is also helped by the light of day. There's a saying, "Sunlight is the greatest disinfectant." And that means that when anything (circumstance, situation, relationship...) is exposed to the light of day (pulled out from under the rug, talked about, shared openly after pretending everything's been okay when it hasn't...), we can have greater confidence that what we see is honest and real. Falsehoods, mistakes, deceits...they're all clearly visible.

It makes total sense when we think about what thrives in the shadows, hidden in the dark: dishonesty, anything we're not proud of, secrets, buried truths... And once these are exposed to the light of day, they can't hide anymore. Their true nature is clear, and we can face them with courage and confidence that we know what we're dealing with.

## Face it and grow

Facing something we'd rather not almost always will take us outside our comfort zones, outside our safe, familiar space into an area where things get...weird. Where lines are thin and crooked. Where we stumble and fall. Where we've said yes to something for the first time, and we're not good at it. It feels wobbly and we will struggle. Our first efforts at something will be tilted and uneven – far from perfect.

But you know what, beautiful someone? Not only is wobbly okay, it's great because when we wobble, we have to figure out what to do to steady ourselves. When things feel weird, we have to learn how to make them feel...normal. When our cake, crocheted llama, or row of garden basil comes out gnarled and curly, we have to figure out how to straighten it out and in the process, learn a whole lot about what doesn't work. When we wobble, we grow.

So let's turn to face it, whatever it is, or try it, whatever that means. Let's wobble and not be afraid.

And while we wobble, let's turn off the noise — whether that's opinions or articles or "experts" or headlines. Let's tell them to shush. We're trying to grow here. We can't be distracted by every click that comes our way.

## Step back

We read about a tragic accident, hear about a neighbor's illness, or see pictures of refugees who've lost everything, and pause, filled with sadness and pain for them. We promise ourselves we'll remember what's important, go straight home after work to spend time with our kids, text a friend, "Talk soon, okay?"...all good intentions.

But amid the daily pressures of our lives, we soon forget. We (okay I) go back to bellyaching about inconsequential things like traffic or running out of grapefruit or losing the remote. We get caught up in the moments of our day, the petty arguments, the rude waiter or the wilted salad at a restaurant, the overpriced plumber who has us over a barrel because they're the only ones who work on Sundays they explain as the water rises in the kitchen. We're stressed because we allow the small stuff to creep in and rob us of our natural compassion and appreciation for every gift in our lives.

One simple inspiration: we can step back for perspective on what needs facing and what's a passing annoyance. Claude Monet created hundreds of paintings of the water lilies in his garden at Giverny. These works are on display in museums in Paris and New York. Monet's idea was to create large expanses (he called them *grandes decorations*) of his gardens' flowers and streams, working with light, to pull us in to this magnificent landscape.

But here's the thing: it's impossible to appreciate this beauty and understand the scope and magnificence of these works standing two inches from the paintings (of course we're not allowed to get that close to these masterpieces anyway ☺). We've got to stand back to take it all in, appreciate the colors, the use of light, the subtle changes from one part of the painting to the next. And we seem to know this intuitively. We naturally step back a few feet or more in order to get some perspective. And it's interesting…the definition of perspective is actually the ability to see elements clearly *in relation to one another*. It requires a stepping back so that we have a vantage point that enables us to what elements are larger, smaller, brighter, softer?

Applying this to our lives…stepping back for perspective enables us to see which issues we're facing are more or less important, more or less urgent, maybe insignificant? And in doing so, it will likely make them easier to face, or enable us to face them with stronger and more targeted solutions. Perspective calms us down. It lets us take a breath and a clear-eyed look at that thing we're trying so hard to avoid facing: it may very well not be as big and bad as we think.

The distance from the problem alone gives us a fresh perspective on it. We can see it more clearly, unencumbered. We can be less stressed and more relaxed and focused. We can have more honest communication with ourselves about what we are dealing with. We step back and suddenly...

- The solution to a problem is crystal-clear.
- We can envision a solid next step to take.
- We realize the problem isn't that big a deal in the scheme of things.
- We're refreshed and feel more confident that we're talented enough, strong enough, and smart enough to rise to the challenge.
- We remember the last time we handled a tough situation and get a surge of readiness to tackle this one.

So let's step back from our routines on a regular basis, especially if we're feeling the urge to blow things out of proportion or procrastinate about something important. Some of the most powerful revelations happen when we take ourselves away from circumstances for a healthy dose of perspective. There is almost magical power in pausing to relax and refocus. We return to any challenge stronger than when we left. Our mind has continued to work on a problem, even though we're not consciously focused on it.

### Five-minute vacations

It may not be possible to get far away, or even to get away at all. We can still take breaks for walks, trips to the library (a wonderful, quiet oasis), drives through beautiful areas, museums, a long sit at the park with a good book. If even this isn't possible, practice the five-minute vacation. Go outside or sit in the kitchen, close your eyes and picture the most beautiful scene. A place you visited or would like to visit. Take five minutes to picture yourself there, alone or with people you love. Breathe the sweet air, savor the scene in every way you can. You will emerge renewed and refreshed.

Get outside and breathe every day. Go for a walk or bike ride if possible.

Take some deep breaths. Drop your shoulders. Relax your back and chest muscles.

Look at the sky.

Smell the roses.

Hold a baby, kitten, or puppy. Play with kids and celebrate their smiles and giggles.

Get up before dawn once a week to watch the sunrise and enjoy the morning light. It's clean and clear, and also full of the promise of a fresh start, another chance, a page to turn. I love this verse from Percy Bysshe Shelley's poem, *On Love*:

*In the motion of the very leaves of spring, in the blue air, there is then found a secret correspondence with our heart.*

When we get away and stop clenching our brain cells around a challenge, ideas flow, along with rivers of relief.

## Vent to someone you trust
- "I need to get this off my chest."
- "Something's weighing on my mind."
- "We've got to get this out of the way so we can move on."

We talk about frustrations and disappointments as concrete, physical burdens. It's like we know intuitively that these are real barriers pinning us down or blocking the way forward. And while we try to handle things ourselves, there's a limit to the number of times we can do that without needing to vent to someone we trust.

Like the figure of Sisyphus in Greek mythology who strains to push his rock up the hill only to have it roll back down on him, at some point shouldering a burden alone is just too much of a strain. Venting gives voice to what's going on in our head and heart. As we talk with complete abandon, unworried and unhurried to someone we trust, an escape valve opens to release negative, unproductive thoughts, enable us to face an issue squarely and see new possibilities and fresh starts.

Ciara, definitely one of the most balanced people I know, will sometimes call and say, "Okay, I need to complain. For the next five minutes, I don't want to hear anything constructive. I need to get this off my chest, so I'm going to let it rip. Ready?"

Beautiful someone, venting is so important that I encourage you to try it, even if you're the type of person who likes to keep things to yourself.

Venting helps us face it by releasing the negative energy created by the fear, frustration, or anger swirling around in our heads. It also gives us the chance to have our feelings validated, find encouragement, and get constructive ideas for moving ahead from someone we trust.

Sometimes, nothing beats just talking it out, one to one.

DIANA DAVIN

# Create your joy

> Creativity is inventing,
> experimenting, growing,
> taking risks, breaking rules,
> making mistakes,
> and having fun.
>
> — Mary Lou Cook

Max had faced serious emotional challenges in his life, including a long struggle with clinical depression. One thing always seemed to help him: working with horses. One day while making fanciful Playdough horses with his nephew, Max realized just how much these magnificent animals brought him a deep peace he never felt anywhere else in his life.

That afternoon served as the spark of an idea: Max decided to offer workshops where people suffering with depression, going through recovery, or experiencing emotional distress would build the musculature of a horse, layering it piece by piece onto a small skeleton until they had created the entire animal.

One of his favorite sayings was, "The mind cannot forget what the hands have done." And in that I understood what he meant: there was a deep peace participants felt working with their hands, along with a sense of empowerment from what they could create: an entire magnificent animal. This was a process they could never read or hear about or see someone else do — it was something they had to render for themselves and in doing so, experience sanctuary and unique understanding.

Have you had this feeling? After you've made a cake, or planted an herb garden, or played around with your guitar just riffing the beginning notes to a song, or built something in your woodshop?

Author Brenda Ueland wrote sensitively about the incredible importance of personal expression. From her book *If You Want to Write* published in 1938:

> Everybody is talented because everybody who is human has something to express. Try not expressing anything for 24 hours and see what happens. You will nearly burst. You will want to write a long letter or draw a picture or sing or make a dress or a garden. ...[W]riting or painting is putting these thoughts on paper. Music is singing them.
>
> ...This joyful, imaginative, impassioned energy dies out of us very young. Because we do not see that it is great and important. Because we let dry obligation take its place. Because we don't respect it in ourselves and keep it alive by using it. And because we don't keep it alive in others by listening to them.

### *"Because you haven't written it yet"*

During a talk on the process of creating art, writer and producer Julia Cameron, prolific author of *The Artist's Way* series, was asked, "Why should we try to write when true originality isn't really possible? Because really all of the themes and plots that we read are only retreads or adaptations of work that has already been written?" That's the question that every writer and probably every artist asks, particularly because we are by nature self-critical to a fault. Julia's response was simply, "Because <u>you</u> haven't written it yet." With gentle sensitivity, she was saying that every individual creative effort is unique, regardless of the subject being covered, because each artist is different. He or she will have a one-of-a-kind — literally a once-in-the-universe — take on the topic being expressed.

We'll use our own beauty and uniqueness of expression to create something brand new. The world has never seen that before because we've never been here before. And in a very real way, we owe it that. It's our responsibility to be honest and brave enough to share our unique gifts while we're here. The world will make room for our gifts. The world wants our unique contribution while we're here. It's one reason we ARE here. To give and in doing so to feel fulfilled, valued, and happy...and hopefully to inspire someone else to do the same.

There is an inherent creativity in each of us. (Yes, there is!) We are unique, we know this. No one has ever been here before with our one-of-a-kind combination of family, circumstances, talents, and way of seeing the world. We all spent time as children creating: with mud, fingerpaints, crayons, pots and wooden spoons, yarn, clay, and more.

Our hands and minds got busy the moment we saw any blank "canvas": sand, puddles, blank paper, an open cabinet filled with pots and pans — musical instruments just waiting to happen ☺. And here's the thing: we never worried if what we created was "good," a productive use of time, or marketable. We created something for the pure joy of creating it. There was no question in our minds about whether it was worth doing. We just did it.

## Why creativity in a book about living boldly?

"Creativity takes courage," said master French painter Henri Matisse. It definitely does take courage to dance and sing and paint when we feel like we can't. We don't know how, and even if we do, we're not "good" at it. One look at the stores on Etsy, at what people are creating, or anyone whose work is on display at a gallery or museum, or dancers online or on stage is enough to stop us. We could never...

But, beautiful someone, we *can*.

Yeah, we can.

We can move our feet to music. We can open our mouths and make sounds to musical notes. We can put pencil to paper and draw lines. We can look through the lens of a camera, find a gritty urban scene, and capture it in a compelling composition.

These are creative acts that boldly tap an honest, unguarded part of our brains. They transport us to a new place in our hearts — a generous and brave one.

Creativity makes us courageous — trust me, it takes courage to try something outside our normal realm of activity, especially something that requires us to flex creative muscle. When I decided to learn to draw, I took a class at a community arts center nearby. Instantly I fell in love with the surroundings and the feeling of artistry and ingenuity. I loved the smell of the paints and the clay and the pastels. The canvas and the pencils and erasers.

I loved it all right away and wanted so much to be part of it even though I felt like a total poser, an imposter. I mean honestly, *me*? Consultant, businessperson, corporate communicator? Seriously? But I wouldn't let the imposter syndrome take over. The best part about beginning is that you have no ego, so there's nothing to lose. No one knew me. They didn't know my history or my career choices up until then. The community was unbelievably welcoming and open, and I will always be grateful for that. I credit my ability to put pencil to paper and persist in learning to draw to their openness and belief that anyone can create art.

But some of that courage had to come from me, to wit: the day our subject was a Grecian marble bust. I had been taking class at this point for a few months, and if you've ever taken an art class, you know that the way it works is that your easel faces you. The subject is in the middle, and everyone draws what they see from their perspective. The teacher goes around and gives you encouraging feedback and suggestions as you work.

At the end of the class, everyone turns their easel around and shares what they've created. While I was working on my Grecian bust, I thought it was a fair representation of what I was looking at, that is until we all turned our easels around, and I realized that mine honest-to-goodness looked like a crayon drawing in a sea of DaVincis.

It was a day when I wasn't feeling particularly brave. I slithered off vowing never to go back. What was I doing?! I had no business trying to learn to draw. I cried in the parking lot, with the sting of embarrassment in my throat. If it weren't for my instructor texting over and over to encourage me to come back, I'm not sure I would have.

## A miracle

Creativity is truly a miracle that does so much more than challenge us. It also strengthens us to resist judgment. It teaches us to detach from people around us who say things like:

"Why are you trying that? You're not exactly artistic."
"Okay, what IS that?"
"You're still working on that?"
"How much are you spending on those supplies?"
"Are you gonna try to sell that?"
"Why are you wasting time on that when you could be [*fill in the blank*]?"

We gently but firmly t'ai chi any unsupportive comments out of our way with a simple, "I'm enjoying myself" or "It's not for sale" or just offer a knowing and indulgent smile. Remember the words of one of the greatest musical artists of all time, John Lennon, who said, "I always thought there was something wrong with me because I seemed to see things other people didn't see." Thankfully, one day he realized this was just not the case, and "wrong" became wonderful.

Creativity is also a road to personal discovery unlike any other, full of its own serendipitous rewards. In the process of creating something new, we discover what works and what doesn't. We learn how to improvise when things don't go as planned and maybe sometimes uncover an even better idea or approach. We learn about ourselves. Build patience because creating something almost always occurs in stages and learning a craft of any kind definitely takes time. We begin to understand the power of patience and the importance of being satisfied with slow, incremental progress.

We don't finish a painting or textile in a single sitting.

A garden takes months to plant and grow, and seasons pass between the end of one and the start of the next.

Learning to play an instrument is a lifelong quest.

Creativity helps us have a sense of humor about our attempts that don't work. I heard recently that world-renowned chef Julia Child used to joke that if the desert doesn't come out even, cover it with whipped cream and serve it anyway!

Creativity can offer tremendous healing, as there are countless stories of people who (like Max) used art...painting or writing music or molding pottery to bypass the intellect and learn what they were feeling, sometimes surprising themselves, able to finally understand their experiences and even heal trauma through their art.

Art and creativity enabled them to reach for truth and ultimately forgiveness.

> "This is my attempt to be the hero of my own history, despite the shame that has been my closest and constant companion all these years. For my daughter – that she may never experience such things. For myself – who survived whole enough to sing out by the grace of my ancestors, my grandma Isabel, music, mystery, and my hometown of Montréal. For our foremothers and ancestors – who endured far worse and still survived... For the ones whose names we will never know. [W]e are living dreams beyond their wildest imaginings."
>
> – Allison Russell from the liner notes to her album,
> *Outside Child*

I read this and wonder about the phrase, "[W]e are living dreams"... Is "living" a verb or adjective in the artist's rendering? Are we actively living our dreams in spite of hardship, or are we walking, living, creative dreams of humans because of our trauma? Maybe it's both...and why not ☺?

Creativity also teaches us to improvise when something doesn't go as planned. We end up with too much yarn at the end of a weaving project...a cool fringe takes shape. The colors in a painting are too bright for a night scene...suddenly the painting's story takes place during a vibrant sunrise. Crepes look more like pancakes, or we added vanilla instead of almond extract to the batter. "Hmmm...okaaaaay then! Where's the maple syrup?"

In study after study, researchers have found clear links between creativity and self-esteem. And it makes sense: in addition to the aha! moments that this time can produce for us, there is a unique feeling of power that comes from standing back, looking at our creation and saying, "I did that," or "I made that," or "I built that." "That's unique and it's uniquely mine. Whether I keep it for myself or give it to the world, it is one-of-a-kind."

## Saori

Creativity teaches us to believe in and trust our uniqueness, our different way of seeing things. In this way, we understand the principle of possibility.

Saori is a type of weaving originated in 1969 by Japanese artist Misao Jo. The word *saori* translates a number of ways, but in practice it means "everything has its own dignity" and "weaving" together. The original idea was to use weaving as an artistic form, as opposed to just productive and functional cloth-making. Saori took patterned hand weaving and turned it into an art form.

Unlike other forms of loom weaving, in Saori, there are no patterns to follow; each cloth is unique. I've heard it described as "beauty without intentions," in a nod to its experimental, freeform approach to discovering beauty as the weaver creates.

Saori weaving is designed around four principles:

1. Consider the differences between people and machines.
2. Be bold and adventurous.
3. Look out through eyes that shine.
4. Inspire one another, and everyone in the group.

My favorite is "Inspire one another," but look at the second principle: *Be bold*. Yes! Courage is literally woven into this approach to creating artistic cloth! Misao Jo knew instinctively that leaving the beaten path to express creativity in color, texture, luminosity, density and more would require courage. We need to be brave, she was saying, but when we are, our brains and our hearts unclench and our originality can shine.

## We create. Full stop.

So right about now, we may be thinking,

"What if it doesn't work?"
"What if I can't learn how to crochet?"
"What if all I can grow is weeds?"
"What if everything I bake burns?"

"What if my weaving looks like something a six-year-old did at summer camp?"

All beside the point, beautiful someone, and that's especially important for us to know. We're always the ones striving for constant improvement and raising the bar on ourselves.

A few (I hope, helpful) thoughts on creativity:

- We create what we create. Full stop. It does not have to be held against any standard of "good" or (God forbid) saleable, i.e., we don't need to make money at what we create.
- Our creations are unique and worthy *because* we created them.
- At some point we might want to learn techniques and build a craft, but we don't have to.
- We don't need to allow anyone to ever see our creations — some will be for-our-eyes-only and most won't be functional or postable.
- We don't have to compete with anyone regarding what we create, especially artists who spend their lives working at their crafts.
- We don't have to get anyone's opinion about what we create, and if they ask, we don't have to answer, especially if the question is something like, "What *is* that?" "What are you making exactly?" "Do you know what you're doing?" "Why don't you go online and watch the people who know what they're doing?" We can just let a smile be our answer or say something noncommittal like, "It's just for me."

We are creating for our own reasons and that creativity is critically important to living bravely and bringing our full and true selves to the world. So try it, make a mess, follow Julia Cameron's advice: relax knowing that it's impossible to get better at something and look good at the same time. Listen to an inner wisdom, the voice of your soul, about colors you like, music you enjoy, recipes that include ingredients you savor. Try a style of dance that you always thought was just beautiful.

Feel the rush of power that comes from not caring what anyone thinks about what you create.

We are listening now to our own inner voices, beautiful someone, and they are genuine, encouraging, and bold.

DIANA DAVIN

# That's all for now!

*Today is where your book begins*
*The rest is still unwritten.*

— Natasha Bedingfield

Beautiful someone, what if today is the day the everything changes for you? What if today you realize that you are braver than you know, stronger than you think, and more valuable than you've ever let yourself believe?

Because nothing in *Braving It* is out of reach for us. It may seem that way because our brave has been hiding behind years of conditioning and tons of clutter that we're having trouble reaching around. But once we clear out the bad memories, unhealthy relationships, preconceived ideas of what and who we should be and are capable of...and fill that space instead with honest, courageous choices, well, as songwriter and singer Natasha Bedingfield sings in her song *Unwritten*,

> *No one else*
> *Can speak the words on your lips*
> *Drench yourself in words unspoken*
> *Live your life with arms wide open*
> *Today is where your book begins*
> *The rest is still unwritten.*

There is hope and possibility in our bravery. A courageous life is something we owe ourselves, and in a very real way, the world.

Don't deprive it of your beauty, creativity, honest reactions, and full heart.

**Here is my wish for you:** that you know, not just believe, but know in your bones that you are talented, worthy, strong, and one-of-a-kind.

And most of all that you are a work in progress, with the courage to create your life, your way.

Blue skies to you, beautiful!
—Diana
diana@blossiesbooks.com
www.blossiesbooks.com

## ABOUT DIANA DAVIN

Hello, Beautiful Someone!

I'm Diana Davin, author and publisher of Blossie's Books.

I live in a rural part of Connecticut where I moved from New York/New Jersey about 8 years ago. My husband Doug and I have two children who are the center of our lives, also two cats, one dog, 12 chickens, 8 quail, and two beehives which we are told means we have 80,000 or so bee babies.

A little more about me:

> **My days:** Writing (a lot), weaving, gardening, working out (a lot).
> **Fav food:** Cheese doodles (I *know*).
> **Beach or mountains?** Oh, definitely both.
> **Life goal:** Never stop starting.
> **Life quote:** Expect nothing. Blame no one. *DO* something.

## Quick story

You know how sometimes you have an honest-to-goodness revelation, a crystal clear insight into a situation, a relationship, a job, who you are? I had one about a year ago.

Early morning. My kitchen. Hot coffee. Laptop open and waiting for inspiration.

*I am addicted to hope.* I just typed it without thinking. *Addicted to hope.* Huh.

I sat with that for a while and decided it's totally true. I can't seem to give up on the idea that we can always create tomorrow the way we want it to be. And this is not some flimsy hope, like what we feel sitting outside on a sunny day when nothing's wrong. It's easy to be hopeful then.

This hope is strong and *active*. It *makes* things happen. And when they don't, it grieves, it learns, and then it shakes the dust off its feet and moves on with better ideas and fresh energy to jump in with both feet and try again.

(And then I write a book about it for you, beautiful someone!)

Write to me at diana@blossiesbooks.com. I so want to hear your awesome story!

www.ingramcontent.com/pod-product-compliance
Lightning Source LLC
LaVergne TN
LVHW011419080426
835512LV00005B/146